MY JOURNEY FOR CHRIST

Choosing the right church

Duane Seuferer

Published in the United States of America

ISBN: 978-1-956741-44-5 (SC)
ISBN: 978-1-956741-45-2 (Ebook)

Duane N. Seuferer
222 West 6th Street
Suite 400, San Pedro, CA, 90731
www.stellarliterary.com

Order Information and Rights Permission:

Quantity sales. Special discounts might be available on quantity purchases by corporations, associations, and others. For details, contact the publisher at the address above.

For Book Rights Adaptation and other Rights Permission. Call us at toll-free 1-888-945-8513 or send us an email at admin@stellarliterary.com.

References:

Matthew Henry's Commentary 1961

Chronological Life Application Bible

MacArthur Study Bible NKJV 1997

NIV Bible 1984

J. Vernon McGee Commentary

Systematic Theology, Wayne Grudem

Christian Beliefs, Wayne Grudem

The New Book of Knowledge. Copyright 1966

Carol Wimmer—1988

Wikipedia—Internet

All quoted Bible verses are from NIV 1984 version unless indicated otherwise.

Contents

Preface

It was a Saturday morning in January of 2015. I was napping at the end of the couch in a laid-back sitting position, and as I started waking up, I saw a shadow figure standing at the other end of the couch by where my wife was sitting. This shadow changed into a man who was completely white—his clothes, his hair, and even his skin. The only thing that wasn't white were his eyes, and they were dark.

He wasn't looking directly at me. Then he turned his head slightly toward me and disappeared. My first thought was that it was Jesus, but later I could hardly believe it. From the time he changed from a shadow to a person was very short, maybe about four seconds. That wasn't much time to remember what someone looked like, especially when awestricken.

I immediately started questioning things, like, he wouldn't appear to a person like me, and he didn't look like the pictures we usually see of Jesus. In pictures I see of Jesus, his nose is perfectly straight. In my vision, his nose had a slight hump at the bridge, and this seemed to keep my attention because his nose wasn't straight like in pictures.

I decided to Google pictures of Jesus. There are many pictures, but no one knows which ones are even close to accurate. I found an image taken from the Shroud of Turin that was the best image of what I saw. All of the images I saw were from the front of the face. I chose an image where I could see a thickness at the bridge of his nose, which might indicate a hump. There is no evidence that these images are even close, but it made me feel better.

I didn't tell anyone for several months because I didn't think anyone would believe me. I didn't even tell my wife. I finally told one of our pastors, and he assured me I shouldn't think it wasn't Jesus. I have no idea why me, but I do believe it was Jesus.

I was still hesitant to tell others until my daughter sent me an article by Oswald Chambers, who said if you see Jesus, you must tell even if they don't believe.

This is in reference to Mark 16:13.

Introduction

I was born and raised in a Catholic family of six boys. Both of my parents were Catholic, so we followed all the Catholic rules: church every Sunday, holy days, Lenten devotions, and all the fasting and abstaining laws. I don't remember anyone complaining profusely about this because we were all raised believing these were the laws of the Church and this is what we had to do. At age twenty-three I got married in the Catholic Church, and after six years of marriage and one child, we got a divorce.

After being single for about ten years, I got engaged to a non-Catholic. I applied for an annulment, but I was told there was a backlog and it would probably be eighteen months for a decision. We decided to get married in her church and get married in the Catholic Church later if the annulment was approved. I wasn't too concerned because I wasn't sure I believed in annulments anyway.

We started going to our own churches, and after eleven months our first child was born. This created a problem as the Catholic Church has infant baptism, and my wife didn't believe in infant baptism. We continued to go to our own churches and sometimes to each other's church.

In the meantime my annulment was approved, but we didn't get married in the church because there were some requirements we didn't like, and I really didn't care anymore.

To make a long story short, after six years and three children, we decided to find a completely different church. I didn't believe I had to be Catholic to be saved, but the Catholic Church was ingrained in me. It has a lot of history and rituals that are somewhat appealing, but I knew history and rituals don't save us. There are teachings in the church I didn't believe or approve of that made it easier to leave. Even in my childhood I had questioned some of the teachings that were taught in our catechism classes.

I needed to compare Catholic and Protestant doctrines and decide which I thought was the most accurate. After trying a few churches, we chose an Evangelical Free Church.

In this book I share some important scriptural principles and Bible verses that I think inactive Catholics and any unchurched people who don't read the Bible need to know. I quoted most of the Bible verses completely for those who don't read the Bible. I will share what I have learned from scripture and my experiences before and after I left the Catholic Church.

I am using *My Journey for Christ* as a possible guideline for anyone who wants to choose a Bible-teaching church for their walk in a Christ-centered life. This book is a blend of five important spiritual areas that I used for choosing a new church and for raising my family in a Christ-centered life. These five areas are: believing the Bible is the absolute word of God, comparing Catholic and Protestant teachings with the Bible, accepting Jesus as our Savior, what a Christ-centered life should include, and a guideline for choosing a Bible-teaching church.

I intend for the information in this book to be solely my beliefs and opinions, and the references I used were strictly to substantiate my beliefs and opinions.

1 Popes of the Catholic Church

My first questions about the Catholic Church were: Did Jesus appoint Peter as the first pope, and are popes infallible?

The Catholic Church claims their popes are infallible and that Saint Peter was appointed the first pope. The church claims St. Peter was appointed pope when Jesus said to him:

And I tell you that you are Peter and on this rock I will build my church, and the gates of Hades will not overcome it. I will give you the Keys of the Kingdom of heaven; whatever you bind on earth will be bound in heaven, and whatever you loose on earth will be loosed in heaven. (Matthew 16:18–19)

There is some controversy about who Jesus was referring to when he said "this rock." The Catholic Church claims Jesus was referring to Peter as the rock. Some theologians think that when Jesus said "this Rock," he was referring to himself. I will quote two Bible verses that would support that theology.

For no one can lay any foundation other than the one already laid, which is Jesus Christ. (1 Corinthians 3:11)

For in scripture it says: "See I lay a stone in Zion, a chosen and precious cornerstone, and the one who trusts in him will never be put to shame." (1 Peter 2:6–8)

Regardless of which is right, Christ's church was built by all the apostles through Christ. Matthew Henry, an eighteenth-century theologian, said, "The church is built upon the foundation of the apostles."

All believers are to teach the gospel to the people and Matthew 16;18 has nothing to do with Peter having power and authority over all the church. In fact, we know more about Paul building Christ's church from his four journeys throughout Europe planting churches than we know about Peter.

In Galatians 1:15–20, Paul says,

But when God who set me apart from birth and called by his grace was pleased to reveal his Son in me so that I might preach him me among the Gentiles, I did not consult any man, nor did I go up to Jerusalem to see those who were Apostles before I was, but I went immediately into Arabia and later returned to Damascus. Then after three years I went to Jerusalem to get acquainted with Peter and stayed with him 15 days. I saw none other, only James the Lord's brother.

We can see by these verses that Paul was preaching the gospel for three years before he ever met Peter. Evidently Peter wasn't head of the church, and later Paul had to correct Peter.

When Peter came to Antioch, I opposed him to his face, because he was clearly in the wrong. Before certain men came from James, he used to eat with the Gentiles. But when they arrived, he began to draw back and separate himself from the gentiles because he was afraid of those who belong to the circumcision group. The other Jews joined him in his hypocrisy, so that by their hypocrisy even Barnabas was led astray. When I saw that they were not acting in line with the truth of the Gospel, I said to Peter in front of them all, “You are a Jew, yet you live a gentile and not like a Jew? How is it then that you force gentiles to follow Jewish customs?” (Galatians 2:11–14)

In these verses we see that Paul had to correct Peter. If Peter was pope and popes are infallible, he certainly didn’t attain that status at this time.

The verse the Catholic Church uses to claim Peter had authority over all the church is Matthew 16:19: “I will give you the keys of the kingdom of Heaven; and whatever you loose on earth will be loosed in Heaven.” The authority to bind and loose laws was not just given to Peter, Jesus gave this same authority to the disciples in Matthew 18:18. This is about binding and loosing the laws of the church. Jesus changed some of the laws of Moses. For example Jesus changed eye for an eye and tooth for a tooth (Matthew 5:38–39) and divorce only in cases of adultery (Matthew 5:32).

I will quote Matthew Henry for the two keys to heaven.

Now the keys of the kingdom of Heaven are, (1) the key of doctrine, called the key of Knowledge. Now the Apostles had an extraordinary power of this kind; some things forbidden by the Law of Moses were now to be allowed; some things allowed there were now to be forbidden and the apostles were empowered to declare this to the world. Christ gives His apostles power to shut or open the Book of the Gospel to people, as the case required. When ministers preach pardon and peace to the penitent, wrath and the curse to the impenitent, in Christ’s name, they act then pursuant to this authority of binding and loosing. (2) The key of discipline, which is but the application of the former to particular persons, upon a right estimate of their characters and actions. Christ’s ministers have a power to admit into the church; "go, disciple all nations, baptizing them; those who profess faith in Christ, and obedience to Him, admit them by baptism."

They have a power to expel and cast out such as have forfeited their church membership. They have a power to restore and receive it again, upon their repentance, such as had been thrown out; to loose those whom they had been bound.

Since I have never read anything in scripture that definitely indicates that Jesus appointed Peter as head of the church and that apostle Paul had to scold him for wrongdoing, I don't believe Peter was appointed head of God's church.

All the apostles except for John were martyred. Christians were severely persecuted, and Christianity was not allowed by the Roman government for over 275 years. I don't know how the popes could manage a church during this time frame.

According to history, when Constantine became emperor of the Roman Empire, he lifted the persecution of Christians with the Edict of Milan in AD 313. Constantine made himself head of the church. He didn't really like Christianity, so he mixed Christian beliefs with Roman pagan beliefs for a new Christian religion. By adding pagan beliefs, this religion would teach things that are not biblical. Two good questions would be: Did some of these pagan beliefs creep into Catholic doctrine, and how can the church claim the church is from Jesus when Constantine made himself head of the church AD 313?

The Catholic Church gives a line of popes from Peter to the present day, but some historians believe the first true pope started with Pope Leo I, in AD 440. Pope Leo I successfully negotiated with the

Huns in AD 452 and the Vandals in AD 455 to not invade Rome. This showed some power in the church, and he also took control of the bishops.

Actually, at this point in time, the head of the church was called the bishop of Rome, and the church didn't use the title "pope" until after the fall of the Roman Empire (AD 493).

As a Catholic, I never heard much about all the problems that occurred throughout the line of popes.

From 1378 till 1417 the Roman Catholic Church went through a period of the Great Western Schism. In this period there were two popes and eventually three popes at the same time.

TRUE POPES	FASLE POPES
1378-1406 POPE URBAN VI	1378 POPE CLEMENT VII
	1389 POP BONIFADE IX
1406-1415 POPE GREGORY XII	1394 POPE BENEDICT XIII
	1409 POPE ALLEXANDER V
1417-1431 POPE MARTIN V	1410 POPE JOHN XXII

In the year 1414 there was the Council of Constance, in which Emperor Sigismund persuaded John XXIII to resign. The council also persuaded Pope Gregory XII, the successor of Pope Urban VI, to resign in 1415. This position of Benedict XIII, who had succeeded Clement VIII, was dismissed. The other false popes had died or been exiled.

Now that they had cleaned house, in 1417 Pope Martin V was elected pope, and the Western Schism was over.

The New Book of Knowledge Encyclopedia lists a number of popes as doubtful, anti-popes, and pretenders. It appears these false and doubtful popes were between the years of AD 217 and AD 1522. It seems as though there were serious political problems periodically during this time frame.

Another serious conflict in the church was Pope Leo X allowing churches to sell indulgences in the year 1517. The churches were selling indulgences for cash, telling people their sins would be forgiven.

Martin Luther, a German Catholic monk, protested the sale of indulgences and was eventually excommunicated from the Catholic Church and became the leader of the Protestant Movement. Luther was right that we can't buy forgiveness of sins as sins are only forgiven by the grace of God.

Luther was the first person to translate and publish the Bible in the German dialect. His New Testament translation was published in 1522 and the Old Testament translation was in 1534, giving the Germans the entire Bible in German.

Martin Luther went on to be recognized by many as a great theologian.

In this day and age, the controversy in the church is about a behind the scenes pope called the Black Pope. The main controversy is whether he is in complete control or just an advisor to the Jesuits.

If you Google "Black Pope" on the Internet, there is also information about three early popes who were descendants of North Africa. They were the fourteenth pope, Pope Victor 189–198, the thirty-second pope, Pope Miltiades, 311–314, and the forty-ninth pope, Pope Gelasius, 492–496. There doesn't seem to be much concrete information, but being from North Africa, it is logical that they were of a black nationality.

The main purpose of this chapter was to give evidence that Jesus never actually made Peter head of his church and give some history about popes that I think indicates they are not infallible.

I think the wrongdoing of Pope Leo X and all the doubtful and anti-popes proves that popes are not infallible.

None of us are perfect as we fall short of the glory of God (Romans 3:23).

2 Saving Grace through Faith

We need to share with our friends Ephesians 2:8–9: "For it is by grace you have been saved, through faith and this not from yourselves, it is the gift of God not by works so that no one can boast."

We gain salvation only by God's grace, which we get by faith in Jesus Christ. All the works in the world will not save us.

Paul tells us in Romans 11:6, "And if by grace, then it is no longer works, if it were, grace would no longer be grace."

If we could work our way to heaven, then Christ died on the cross for nothing.

Isiah 64:6 tells us, "All of us become like on who is unclean, and all our righteous acts are like filthy rags."

Jesus tells us in John 3:15–17 that we must be born again by believing in him:

That everyone who believes in him may have eternal life. For God so loved the world that he gave his one and only son, that whoever believes in him shall not perish but have eternal life. For God did not send his son into the world to condemn the word, but to save the world through him.

If all Mother Theresa had to show were her works, she would not have salvation. Only faith in Jesus can save us. I'm sure she knew Jesus as her Savior. One of her quotes at the Nobel Lecture, December

11, 1979, "Never let anything so fill you with sorrow as to make you forget the joy of the Christ risen."

Her faith in Jesus would be what saved her, and her works will be her blessings in heaven. This doesn't mean works aren't important. Being a good, moral person is important, but we have to first believe in Jesus for salvation. Jesus makes this very clear in John 14:6, where Jesus answered, "I am the way and the truth and the life. No one comes to the father except through me."

I have heard people say that they have been such a terrible person that God wouldn't want them. This couldn't be farther from the truth. God chose the apostle Paul to teach the gospel and write epistles in the Bible. Paul admits that he persecuted God and Christians, but he still became one of the most prolific writers of the New Testament even though he had been a terrible person.

Paul confesses in Galatians, 1 Timothy, and 1 Corinthians how he persecuted Christians and God's church.

Even though I was once a blasphemer and a persecutor and a violent man, I was shown mercy because I acted in ignorance and unbelief. The grace of our Lord was poured out on me abundantly, along with the faith and love that are in Christ Jesus. (Timothy 1:13–14)

For I am the least of the apostles and do not even deserve to be called an apostle, because I persecuted the Church of God. 10 But by the grace of God I am what I am, and his grace to me was not without effect. No, I worked harder than all of them yet not I, but the grace of God that was with me. (1 Corinthians 15:9–10)

When we accept Christ and become Christians, we can expect to be persecuted in some way. In some countries it might be physical punishment and/or prison. In this country it will probably be mostly verbal.

Paul makes it clear in 2 Timothy 3:12 that if we follow Christ we will be persecuted:

In fact everyone who wants to live a Godly life in Christ will be persecuted.

Jesus said in the Sermon on the Mount that we should rejoice and be glad when we are persecuted because great is our reward in heaven. No one likes persecution, and we may need to pray to God for strength to overcome this persecution. Today on social media we see Christians insulted and ridiculed for their beliefs. As Christians we know many of these accusations are lies, but non-Christians may believe them. We must always remember God is in control and keep praying.

Blessed are you when people insult you, persecute you and falsely say all kinds of evil against you because of me. Rejoice and be glad, because great is your reward in heaven, for in the same way they persecuted the prophets who were before you. (Matthew 5:11–12)

Sometimes non-Christians like to remind us about the wrong we did before we became Christians. They like to find fault with Christians and their ministers. I guess non-Christians think Christians are supposed to be perfect.

I will share this poem written by Carol Wimmer in 1988 and first published by Hi-Call Gospel Magazine in 1992.

It gives some good examples of why we Christians do not think we are holier than thou.

I Am a Christian

When I say that "I am a Christian," I am not shouting that "I am clean living." I'm whispering "I was lost, but now I'm found and forgiven."

When I say "I am a Christian," I don't speak of this with pride. I'm confessing that I stumble and need Christ to be my guide.

When I say "I am a Christian," I'm not trying to be strong. I'm professing that I'm weak and need His strength to carry on.

When I say "I am a Christian," I'm not bragging of success. I'm admitting I have failed and need God to clean my mess.

When I say, "I am a Christian," I'm not claiming to be perfect. My flaws are far too visible, but God believes I am worth it."

When I say "I am a Christian," I still feel the sting of pain. I have my share of heartaches, so I call upon His name.

When I say "I am a Christian," I'm not holier than thou. I'm just a simple sinner who received God's good grace somehow!

Like Paul, we can leave our sins with Jesus and let him change our lives. Nonbelievers don't realize that we become new people in Christ.

Therefore, if anyone is in Christ, he is a new creation, the old has gone, the new has come! All this is from God, who reconciled us to himself through Christ and gave us the ministry of reconciliation: that God was reconciling the world to himself in Christ, not counting men's sins against them. (2 Corinthians 5:17–19)

Who (Jesus) gave himself for us to redeem us from all wickedness and to purify for himself for us to redeem us from all wickedness and to purify for himself a people that are his very own, eager to do what is good. (Titus 2:14)

From these verses we know that no matter how much wrong we have done, we can accept Christ, serve him, and be saved. After we accept Christ, people should be able to see a change in our lives.

Some churches emphasize having a "personal relationship with Christ." If I am witnessing to someone, I won't use this phrase for starters because it's not in the Bible. If this person has some knowledge of the Bible, he or she might say, "I haven't seen that in the Bible." In fact, I saw a statement like this in a non-fundamentalist book, which I will be quoting from later. I prefer using we must "trust in the Lord with all your heart" because that phrase is in the Bible.

I don't believe I was ever taught personal relationship or trust in the Lord in my younger years. Here is a list of Bible verses that tell us to trust in the Lord

Trust in the Lord with all your heart and lean not on your own understanding, in all your ways acknowledge him, and he will make your paths straight. (Proverbs 3:5–6)

For it is with your heart that you believe and are justified, and it is with your mouth that you confess and are saved." As scripture says, anyone who trusts in him will never be put to shame. (Romans 10:10–11)

Those who know your name will trust in you, for you, Lord, have never forsaken those who seek you. (Psalm 9:10)

Wayne Gruden in Systematic Theology states it this way: "Saving faith is trust in Jesus Christ as a living person for forgiveness of sins and for eternal life with God."

Trusting in Jesus with all your heart would be a "personal relationship."

We must make sure we are really trusting in Christ. Many people know Jesus was born on Christmas, died on Good Friday, and was raised from the dead on Easter. This is just knowing who Jesus is. Even the demons know who God is. We know this from James 2:19: "You believe that there is one God. Good! Even the demons believe that and shudder." If we put our faith in Jesus, we won't have to shudder.

There are three important steps to faith; knowledge, agreement, and trust. "We must know who God is, agree with his word, and trust in Jesus with all your heart."

If we do these three things and pray to God every day, we will have our salvation.

The following story is from J. Vernon McGee's commentary.

The story is told that the devil had a meeting with his demons to decide how to persuade men that God was nonexistent. Since themselves believed in his existence they wondered just how to do it. One demon suggested that they tell people Jesus Christ never existed and that men should not believe such fiction. Another demon suggested that they persuade men that death ends all and there is no need to worry about life after death. Finally, the most intelligent demon suggested that they tell everyone that there is a God, that there is a Jesus Christ and that believing saves, but all you have to do is profess faith in Christ and go on living in sin as you used to. They decided on this tactic, and it is the tactic the devil uses today

This is an example of people who follow this theory aren't really repenting Christians. We must have an authentic profession of faith and make an honest attempt to stop sinning to obtain salvation.

If you truly accept Christ, you will not lose your salvation. I will quote verses from the gospel of John that verify this.

My sheep listen to my voice: I know them and they follow me. I give them eternal life and they shall never perish, no one can snatch them out of my hand. My father, who has given them to me, is greater than all; no one can snatch them out of my Father's hand. (John 10:27–29)

And this is the will of him who sent me, that I shall lose none of all that he was given me, but raised them up on the last day. For my father's will is that everyone who looks to the son and believes in him shall have eternal life, and I will raise him up on the last day. (John 6:39–40)

If we believe and trust in Jesus, we know we have salvation. First John 15:12–13 tells us this: "He who has the son has life; he who does not have the son of God does not have life. I write these things to you who believe in the name of the son of God so that you know that you have eternal life."

I have never known the Catholic Church to teach you can know you're saved. The way I understood their teachings was if you tried to obey the Ten Commandments and the church laws, you might go to heaven immediately, but more than likely you will have to go to purgatory for a while.

The Catholic Church also doesn't teach that your salvation is locked in.

If you truly accept Christ, you will not lose your salvation or do anything to lose it.

Trust in the Lord with all your heart and lean not on your own understanding; in all your ways acknowledge him, and he will make your paths straight. (Proverbs 3:5–6)

You should know if you're trusting in Christ or not.

I will quote some other scriptures that guarantee our salvation.

For I am convinced that neither death nor life, neither angels nor demons, neither the present nor the future, nor any powers, neither height nor depth, nor anything else in all creation will be able to separate us from the love of God that is in Christ Jesus our Lord." (Romans 8:38–39)

Because of your partnership in the Gospel from the first day until now, being confident of this, that he who began a good work in you will carry it on to completion until the day of Christ Jesus. (Philippians 1:5–6)

Praise be to God and Father of our Lord Jesus Christ in his great mercy he has given us new birth into a living hope through the resurrection of the Jesus Christ from the dead, and into an inheritance that can never perish, Spoil or fade-kept in heaven for you, who through faith are shielded by God's power until the coming of the salvation that is ready to be revealed in the last time. (1 Peter 1:3–5)

These scriptures make it clear that we can't lose our salvation if we have the love of God in us. Hebrews 6:4–6 is sometimes used to indicate that we could lose our salvation.

It is impossible for those who have once been enlightened, who have tasted the Heavenly gift, who have shared in the Holy Spirit, 5 who have tasted the goodness of the Word of God and the powers of the coming age, 6 If they fall away to be brought back to repentance, because to their loss they are crucifying the Son of God all over again and subjecting Him to public disgrace. (Hebrews 6:4–6)

The theologians I researched agree that these verses are not referring to people who have totally accepted Jesus Christ in their hearts.

These verses use the words enlighten, tasted, and shared. It means they never totally bought into the faith of Jesus. This is not losing salvation because they never completely accepted Christ; therefore, they didn't have it to start with.

Paul says he obtained mercy because he sinned out of ignorance and unbelief.

Although I was formerly a blasphemer, a persecutor, and an insolent man; But I obtained mercy because I did it ignorantly in unbelief. 14 And the grace of our Lord was exceedingly abundant, with faith and love which are in Christ Jesus. (1 Timothy 1:13–14)

Some of the Pharisees were an example of rejecting Christ when they knew he was God. We see this in John 11:48: "If we let him go on like this, everyone will believe in him and the Romans will come and take away both our place and our nation."

The Pharisees' position was more important to them than God, so they didn't want people believing in Jesus. They were denying Christ.

This would not pertain to people who are taking time to decide if they are going to accept Christ if they don't reject or blaspheme him in the meantime. I read that if you desire to come back to Jesus, he will let you back. This could be saying that if God is not going to let you back, he will blind you so you don't want back.

3 Works

When we accept Christ as our Savior in our hearts, God will acknowledge our works and give us blessings here on earth and later in heaven. Works before we accept Christ give us self-satisfaction and might make us look good. Some theologians think God gives non-Christians blessings here on earth for their good works. In my opinion, works of nonbelievers only give self-satisfaction.

Jesus does not want anyone prophesizing in his name unless they are living the faith. He refers to these phony believers as "wolves in sheep's clothing." Jesus reminds us to beware of false prophets; "a bad tree bears bad fruit." Jesus is referring to these kinds of people in these next verses.

Jesus said, many will say to me on that day, Lord, Lord, did we not prophecy in your name and in your name drive out demons and perform many miracles? Then I will tell them plainly I never knew you. Away from me you evil doers. (Matthew 7:22–23)

We should also keep our works as secret as possible and not try to impress people with our works. Some works are impossible to keep secret, such as work at church, community work, and work on the mission field. In fact, this is exemplifying a good example. In my opinion, to keep our works secret is let our actions speak not our words.

In John 15:5–6 Jesus tells us we can do nothing apart from him: "I am the vine, you are the branches. If a man remains in me and I in him, he will bear much fruit; apart from me you can do nothing. If anyone does not remain in me, he is like a branch that is thrown into the fire and burned."

I think this verse verifies that we can do nothing without Jesus, and after we accept him, we then begin to bear fruit. Works does not take precedence over faith, but works are a result of faith. I explained previously that once you have salvation, you can't lose it. Using this analogy, some people think we don't have to do any works because our salvation is locked in. Our salvation is locked in if our profession of faith is authentic. If our profession of faith is authentic, we will want to start our works for the love of Christ. How many works we do depends on how many blessings we want here on earth and in heaven. We must first accept Jesus as our Lord and Savior, and then we begin our works for Christ.

We need to obey God's laws and show our appreciation for what Jesus did for us. This will help us grow in faith. Works can give us perseverance against Satan and also see us growing in the fruits of the spirit.

Galatians 5:22–23 says, "But the fruits of the Spirit is love, joy, peace, patience, kindness, gentleness, and self-control."

Remember, we can only receive God's blessings for our godly works after we receive God's grace by professing our faith in Jesus. "Apart from me you can do nothing" (John 15:5).

In Ephesians 6:10–18, the apostle Paul tells us God has works planned in advanced for us.

We are to honor our Fathers and Mothers. We are to put on the full armor of God so that you can take a stand against the devils schemes, and pray in the Spirit on all occasions with all kinds of prayers and requests. Stand firm then, with the belt of truth buckled around your waist, with the breastplate of righteousness In place, and with your feet fitted with readiness that comes from the gospel of peace. In addition to all this, take up the shield of faith, with which you can extinguish all the flaming arrows of the evil one. Take the helmet of salvation and the sword of the Spirit, which is the word of God. And pray in the Spirit on all occasions with all kinds of prayers and requests.

The apostle Paul tells us that husband and wife will become one flesh and we are to bring our children up in the training and instruction of the Lord. Christian parenting is bringing up our children in the instruction of the Lord and could be one of the most important works of our lives. It is important that Dad be head of the family and be supported and encouraged by his wife. Being the head of the family includes being the spiritual leader by taking the family to church, praying with the family, and setting a good Christian example, including respecting his wife. Fathers bringing their children up in the training and the instruction of the Lord (6:4) is not only raising our children in Christ, but make sure we are living in Christ. Your children will remember your teachings the rest of their lives.

My son, keep your Fathers commands and do not forsake your Mothers teachings. Bind them upon your heart forever;

fasten them around your neck. When you walk, they will guide you; when sleep, they will watch over you, when you awake they will speak to you. (Proverbs 6:20–22)

Studies have shown that when Dad doesn't go to church, only about 15 percent of their sons will attend church when they become adults. This indicates how important Dad's example is. Usually dads don't have to be told to play with their sons as sons usually have an electric train and a remote car soon after they learn to walk. Dad should keep a good relationship at least through high school and at best a lifetime. Good relationship builders can be Cub Scouts, Boy Scouts, 4H, sports, music, camping, and church activities, to name a few. If they belong to one of the organizations I mentioned, make sure the leaders are good moral people. Try and find people who know them and ask questions.

Dads also need to have a close relationship with their daughters from infant through their teen years. This should start early on with things like pretend tea parties and playing with her other girl toys. If you are having a pretend tea party, make sure you are paying attention. I read a story about a dad having a pretend tea party with his little daughter. She was using water for pretend tea, and he was watching TV and not paying too much attention. It finally dawned on him, "Where is she getting this water?" A convenient place—the toilet. We should pay attention.

Dad should also have an interest in all her activities through high school and into her adult world. Girls love their daddies and need them to be there for them. This will have an influence on her self- esteem, self-image, and confidence and possibly how she chooses her husband. I have also read that it is important for dads to like their children's pets, even if it's a goldfish.

Mothers should nurture their children in the Lord with prayers and teaching the children to pray about their problems. My wife would tell our children to "pray about it." If their prayers weren't answered in the way they wanted, she would tell them it wasn't meant to be. This was very important in teaching our children to pray for things but not always expect the answer they wanted. It must be in God's will. Mothers should teach by example in the Lord and teach their children to always be respectful and honest to other people. Mothers should teach their children about Jesus and how to accept him as their Savior. Dads need to help with these duties also.

Mothers should also be interested in their activities and always be there for them and most are. Mothers have a special kind of bonding with their children that Dad's don't have.

Some of these relationships I have grouped together for Dad and Mom are interchangeable if necessary. Examples would be if a parent travels, is in the military, or has a difficult work schedule. Try to keep Mom and Dad in their roles.

I have heard of parents who don't make their children go to church because it might cause them to hate church. It will probably cause them to like staying home. Children will try to control their parents, but parents must have the control.

Train a child in the way he should go, and when he is old he will not turn from it. (Proverbs 22:6)

Take them to church!

It is very important that husband and wife work together and not against each other. This would include when and how to discipline. If husband and wife don't work together, the children will see this and destroy your discipline. Satan works very hard at destroying families and unfortunately is very successful at it. The divorce rate is about 50 percent. Parents need to pray for their children every day of their lives from the day they are conceived. We need to be praying families. Many times I needed to follow my own advice in parenting.

Do not be anxious about anything, but in every situation, by prayer and petition, with thanksgiving present your requests to God. And the peace of God, which transcends all understanding, will guard your hearts and minds in Christ Jesus. (Philippians 4:6–7)

Praying, keeping Jesus at the center of our marriages, and asking what would Jesus do should be all the marriage counseling we need.

Other works God has prepared for us will flow after we have accepted Jesus as our Savior. When God tugs at our heart to do a work, we might try to reject the work, but sometimes God keeps tugging. Satan will try to keep us from doing God's work. We need to stay in prayer about it. I believe if God wants us to do a work, we won't be able to ignore the tug at our heart. I have heard it said that God has a unique plan for each and every one of us. We also need to pray to know what our spiritual gifts are.

We have different gifts according to the grace given us. If a man's gift is prophesying, let him use it in proportion to his faith. If it is serving, let him serve, if it is teaching, let him teach; if it is encouraging, let him encourage; if it is contributing to the needs of others, let him give generously; if it is leadership, let him govern diligently; if it is showing mercy, let him do it cheerfully. (Romans 12:6–8)

Some of our works can be a matter of obedience. God has always demanded obedience from the beginning of the human race. He demanded obedience from Adam and Eve not to eat from the tree of life. He gave Moses the Ten Commandments and punished the Israelites for their disobedience. Through scripture Jesus has given us the two great commandments and the Great Commission:

Jesus replied, love the Lord your God with all your heart and with all your soul and all your mind. This the first and greatest commandment. And the second is like it: Love your neighbor as yourself. All the law and the prophets hang on these two commandments. (Matthew 22:37–40)

Therefore, go and make disciples of all nations, baptizing them in the name of the Father and of the Son, and of the Holy Spirit, and teaching them to obey everything I have commanded you. And surely, I am with you always, to the very end of the age. (Matthew 28:19–20)

This commission is one of the indications of the Trinity and also that we need to be baptized. This also informs us we need missionaries teaching in all parts of the world. Jesus said that the gospel will be preached to all nations before the end of times.

And this Gospel of the Kingdom will be preached in the whole world as a testimony to all nations, and then the end will come." (Matthew 24:14)

This doesn't mean we all have to be missionaries and travel the world. We can be missionaries right in our own communities and serve God in many different capacities. As I wrote earlier, God may tug at our hearts. I will quote verses from 1 John that make it very clear we are to obey God and walk as Jesus did:

The man who says I know him, but does not do what he commands is a liar and the truth is not in him. But if anyone obeys his word, God's love is truly made complete in him. This is how we know we are in him. Whoever claims to live in him must walk as Jesus did. (1 John 2:4–6)

This is how we know who the children of God are, and who the children of the devil are: Anyone who does not do what is right is not a child of God, nor is anyone who does not love his brother. (1 John 3:10)

Those who obey his commands live in him, and he in them. (1 John 3:24)

"And this is how we know that he lives in us: We know it by the spirit he gave us."

We had better choose to obey God and have some works for our fruits as Jesus said in the Sermon on the Mount.

A good tree cannot bear bad fruit and a bad tree cannot bear good fruit, every tree that does not bear good fruit is cut down and thrown into the fire. (Matthew 7:18–19)

Don't take works wrong. This all about our faith producing works after we have professed a true faith in Jesus and obtained our salvation. We must do this first and foremost before we do our works. Works cannot, will not, and never will pay the price for our sins. Only the blood of Christ will cleanse our souls of all of our sins. When we have Jesus in our hearts, we should follow our hearts. The church hymn "Trust and Obey says, "Trust and obey for there's no other way." That says it all. I am writing some quotes from three theologians I have been researching.

Matthew Henry says, "Faith is the root, good works are the fruits and we must see to that we have both. We must not think that either without the other will justify and save us."

McArthur Study Bible Footnote: "Just as professed compassion without action is phony. The kind of faith without works is mere empty profession, not genuine saving faith. … We are saved by grace from a genuine profession of faith to Jesus, a profession of faith that will produce works." Wayne Grudem, in Christian Beliefs, says, "While those who are truly Christians will persevere to the end, only those who persevere to the end are truly Christians. In John 8:31, Jesus says, "If you abide in my word, you are truly my disciples." One evidence of genuine faith is continuing to believe and obey what Jesus said and commands. A perfect life is not necessary, but a true Christian's life will continue to show a general pattern of obedience to Christ's commands and an imitation of his life."

4 Does James Contradict Paul?

People who believe in works for salvation like to use James 2:17 for their argument: "In the same way faith by itself if not accompanied by action is dead."

They must think James is contradicting Paul in Ephesians 2:8. The Bible does not contradict itself.

Second Timothy 3:16–17 says, "All scripture is God breathed and is useful for teaching, rebuking, correcting, and training in righteousness, so that the man of God may be thoroughly equipped for every good work." The best proof the Bible is from God is the New Testament fulfills the prophecies of the Old Testament. This couldn't be a coincidence.

If the Bible appears to contradict itself, you are not interpreting it right. No one has ever proved the Bible wrong. I have heard some say the Bible is just a guideline. It is the absolute word of God. We must not add or detract anything from God's word.

I warn everyone who hears the words of prophecy of this book: If anyone adds anything to them, God will add to him the plagues described in this book. And if anyone takes words away from this book of prophesy, God will take away from him his share in the tree of life and in the holy city, which are described in this book. (Revelation 22:18–19)

In an anti-fundamentalist book the author said the Catholic Church chooses to fully follow James's advice in 2:14–17. Is he indicating that James and Paul disagree? Really, they don't.

In a previous chapter he used 1 Corinthians 1:14–16 to try and prove there is humanity in scripture and is not always God breathed: "I am thankful that I did not baptize any of you except Crispus and Gains. So no one can say that you were baptized into my name. Yes, I also baptized the household of Stephanas; beyond that, I do not remember if I baptized anyone else."

The author was trying to make the point that if the Bible was dictated by God, God would not have had a loss of memory of who Paul baptized. God did not forget who or how many people Paul baptized. God is saying Paul did not remember how many people he baptized. The next verse shows that Paul was only concerned about his mission to preach the gospel and not to remember how many people he baptized.

First Corinthians 1:17 says, "For Christ did not send me to baptize, but to preach the gospel, not with words of human wisdom, lest the cross of Christ be emptied of its power."

Paul's main objective was to be sure the people understood and believed in the power of the crucifixion, not how many he could baptize.

Getting back on track, James is not contradicting Paul because he is saying that works shows the strength of our faith. If you have no works, you have no strength and your faith is dead. If you have no works, your profession of faith was probably phony to start with.

I will quote J. Vernon McGee's commentary about phony faith:

The faith that James is talking here is professing faith which is phony and counterfeit. Paul refers to the same idea when he says in 1 Corinthians 15:2, "unless ye have believed in vain," Paul also wrote, "Examine yourselves, whether ye be in faith …" 2 Corinthians 13:5.

McGee quotes James 2:10, "For whosoever shall keep the whole law and yet offend in one point, he is guilty of all." McGee goes on to say, "As someone has put it, 'Man cannot be saved by perfect obedience, for he cannot render it. He cannot be saved by imperfect obedience, because God will not accept it." The only solution to this dilemma is the redemption that is in Christ Jesus, and both James and Paul emphasize that."

We are saved by grace through faith not by works. If we could work our way to heaven Christ died for nothing. Scripture makes it very clear faith must come first and then produces works that are very important to show our faith is authentic.

5 Sacraments of the Catholic Church

In chapter 2 we learned or were reminded we are saved by grace through faith, not by works, as stated in Ephesians 2:8–9. Paul also tells us in Romans to confess with our mouths and believe in our hearts.

That if you confess with your mouth Jesus is Lord, and believe in your heart that God raised him from the dead, you will be saved. For it is with your heart that you believe and are justified, and it is with your mouth that you confess and are saved. (Romans 10:9–10)

The Catholic Church used to teach that grace was received through the sacraments of the church. All sacraments are works, and we cannot get saving grace from works.

And if by grace, then it's no longer by works, if it were, grace would no longer be grace. (Romans 11:6)

If we could work our way to heaven, then Christ suffered and died for nothing. I realize there are Catholics who are born again by accepting Christ as their Lord and Savior from reading the Bible or some other source. I know there are many Catholic Bible studies that have been started. When I was young Catholic, Bible studies were unheard of.

Some Catholics believe the Vatican II Council in 1963 and 1964 changed a lot of their old teachings. According to my research, the Vatican II Council did not change Catholic doctrine. It did change methods and precepts, of which the majority was in the Mass. The alters were changed, mass no longer had to be said in Latin, communion could be received in the hand, and people could receive both elements on special occasions. The council also changed how Protestants would be regarded. Catholics would no longer call Protestant's heretics but call them separated brethren. These are only a few of the many changes, but I can't see how the Catholic Church could ever change their basic doctrine because that would be admitting that their popes were not infallible and that the church was not from Jesus and the apostles.

In my research I used a Catholic catechism that stated it was updated and revised to meet the teaching of the Second Vatican council. I will paraphrase some statements from this catechism. Christ gives grace to each soul through the Catholic Church by the sacraments. The grace of Christ is attained in the soul by these sacraments.

Sacraments can't give grace because sacraments are works and grace is a gift.

I understand that the Catholic Church now acknowledges they are justified by faith and good works must flow from this faith. I am not sure, but I think they are teaching the sacraments are needed to finish the salvation process. I was taught nothing like this when I went to catechism. We were taught we were saved by sanctifying grace from the sacraments of the church.

My question is, how can the Catholic Church change their teachings when they have taught for hundreds of years that this is Jesus's church and the popes are infallible? It also appears they are deviating from the updated Vatican II catechism.

The seven sacraments of the church are:

Baptism

Confirmation

Penance

Holy Eucharist

Extreme unction—last rites

Matrimony

Holy Orders

Only six sacraments are attainable because if you become a priest, you can't marry and vice versa.

Baptism

The Catholic Church teaches that babies should be baptized as soon as possible because baptism takes away original sin, and they can't enter heaven with original sin. It also teaches that if a baby dies before he or she is baptized, the soul wouldn't go to heaven but instead would go to a place called limbo. Limbo is a place of natural happiness but is not heaven, and they wouldn't see God. I have seen nothing in scripture about a place called limbo or anything described as such.

The church also teaches that a baby receives grace for the first time when it's baptized. This can't be saving grace because we can only get saving grace by professing our faith in Jesus, and babies can't profess faith. It is good to dedicate our babies to God, but since babies can't repent and profess their faith, I don't believe in infant baptism. Children should profess faith in God once they fully understand what faith really means. There is no certain age this should happen as every child is different.

If a child dies before he or she is old enough to accept Christ as his or her savior, he or she would probably go to heaven as Jesus said in Matthew 19:14, “Let the little children come to me, and do not hinder them, for the kingdom of heaven belongs to such as these.”

We can’t judge salvation as I will explain in chapter 10, but I think if a child dies it’s best to assume he or she is in heaven.

I believe in adult baptism by immersion as it symbolizes the death and resurrection of Christ.

Going under water symbolizes Jesus being buried in our sins, and rising up out of the water symbolizes Jesus rising from the grave giving us new life.

As soon as Jesus was baptized, He came up out of the water.’ Matthew 3;16.

Usually before a baptism the person makes a profession of faith. This gives him or her saving grace, and this baptism is the baptism of the Holy Spirit. We can make this profession of faith anytime, not just when we are baptized. I don’t believe water baptism alone saves us because that is a work, but it is an element of obedience and identifying with Christ. It is a sign of obedience that we are declaring our faith in Jesus Christ. Jesus himself was baptized to fulfill righteousness as he had no original sin. Baptism is important.

Jesus gives us a command of obedience in Matthew 28:18–20, “All authority in heaven and on earth has been given to me. Therefore go and make disciples of all nations, baptizing them in the name of the father and of the son, and of the Holy Spirit, and teaching them to obey everything I have commanded you. And surely I am with you always to the very end of the age."

Confirmation

Confirmation is the sacrament in which the church teaches that the Holy Spirit comes into the soul and gives them strength to be a good Catholic.

For this sacrament the church uses the scripture Acts 8:16–17, "Because the Holy Spirit had not come on any of them; they had simply been baptized in the name of the Lord Jesus. Then Peter and John placed their hands on them, and they received the Holy Spirit."

This scripture does not make Catholic confirmation scriptural.

Penance

Penance is the sacrament of the forgiveness of sins by confessing them to a Catholic priest and receiving a penance to do for their sins. I will explain more about confession in chapter 7.

Holy Eucharist

This is the sacrament of communion. The church doctrine says the priest has the spiritual power to change the bread into the physical body of Jesus and the wine into his blood, but it will not have the appearance or taste of flesh and blood. The word the church uses for this is *transubstantiation*. I have never read anything in scripture that says anyone could change bread and wine into the body and blood of Jesus. Even Jesus was talking in symbolic spirit when he said, "Eat my body and drink my blood."

To illustrate that Jesus was speaking in spirit, I will use the scripture from when manna came from heaven.

I am the living bread that came down from heaven. If anyone eats of this bread, he will live forever. This bread is my flesh, which I will give for the life of the world. Then the Jews began to argue sharply among themselves. How can this man give us flesh to eat? Jesus said to them, "I tell you the truth, unless you eat the flesh of the Son of Man and drink his blood you have no life in you. Whoever eats my flesh and drinks my blood has eternal life, and I will raise him up at the last day. For my flesh is real food and my blood is real drink. Whoever eats my flesh and drinks my blood remains in me and I in him.

Just as the living Father sent me and I live because of the Father so the one who feeds on me will live because of me. This is the bread that came down from heaven. Your forefathers ate manna and died, but he who feeds on this bread will live forever. On hearing it, many of his disciples said, "This is a hard teaching. "Who can accept it?" Aware that his disciples were grumbling about this Jesus said to them, "Does this offend you? What if you see the son of man ascend to where he was before!

The spirit gives life; the flesh counts for nothing. The words I have spoken to you are spirit and they are life. Yet there are some of you who do not believe." (John 6:51–64)

In these verses Jesus said, "You must eat the flesh of the son of man and drink his blood."

Then the disciples said this is a hard teaching and who can accept it.

Then Jesus explains it to them: “The spirit gives life, the flesh counts for nothing. The words I have spoken you are spirit and they are life.”

The words Jesus spoke at the Last Supper are the same as he spoke about the manna from heaven. Since he was speaking in spirit about manna, this would indicate that he was also speaking in spirit at the Last Supper. All the apostles were present at the Last Supper. When Jesus said to them, “Do this in remembrance of me.” It would be obvious to me that he was speaking in terms of spirit, not that you are eating my flesh and drinking my blood.

As a Catholic I heard comments from non-Catholics that by saying the “Sacrifice of the Mass” that Catholics were crucifying Jesus all over again. Jesus made the only and last sacrifice on the cross, and right before he died he said, “It is finished” (John 19:30).

The Catholic Church teaches that the communion of bread and wine when consecrated at the mass are changed into the actual body and blood of Christ. Does this make Catholics cannibals? If communion becomes the physical body and blood of Christ but there is no flesh and blood, wouldn’t this be spirit?

I think most Catholics probably think of communion in the spirit form, but this is not what the actual doctrine states.

For years members of the congregation only received the bread at mass except on special occasions. The church wasn’t being precise as Jesus said, “Eat my body and drink my blood.” Again, I believe he was speaking in terms of symbolic spirit.

In my instructions for first communion, the nun told the class not to chew the host with our teeth when we received it because this was

Jesus. We were instructed to let it dissolve until we could swallow it. Did the apostles not chew the unleavened bread at the last supper?

The nun also told us that after we receive communion to go back to our pew and ask Jesus into our hearts. This is what we should do, but what she failed to do was explain what asking Jesus into our hearts really meant. At eight years old I thought I would just say, "Come into my heart." Asking Jesus into our hearts means putting Jesus at the center of our lives.

The heart is the center of our body and is what makes our whole body function. When a baby is born, the heart must be functioning for the breathing process to begin. When we trust in Jesus as our Savior and make him the center of our lives and let him work in our lives, then our spiritual process begins. This is why we say, "asking Jesus into our hearts." Trust in the Lord with all your heart (Proverbs 3:5).

I heard this statement in a Sunday sermon: "The heart is the core of a person's well-being, the source of your life, and the direction of your life." You better have Jesus in this heart.

Extreme Unction

This sacrament is also known as the "last rites." The church teaches this sacrament gives grace to the soul and sometimes strength to the body. It can only be administered by a Catholic priest in the case of a serious accident or serious illness. The church may have become more lenient on these restrictions in recent years. The teachings of the church claims it takes away all venial sins and in certain circumstances mortal sins. The church uses James 5:13–16:

Anyone of you in trouble? Is anyone happy? Let him sing songs of peace. Is anyone of you sick? He should call the elders of the church to pray over him and anoint him with oil in the name of the Lord. And the prayer offered in faith will make the sick person well; the Lord will raise him up. If he has sinned he will be forgiven. Therefore confess your sins to each other and pray for each other so that you may be healed. The prayer of a righteous man is powerful and effective.

How can the Catholic Church state only a priest can perform this when the Bible states that the elders of the church are called to pray and anoint the oil? The Catholic Church doesn't have elders. I think the church says that the priest represents the elders. Priests don't qualify as elders as described in the qualifications of elders in 1 Timothy 3:2–10.

The Catholic Bible does use the term *bishop* instead of elder, but it has basically the same qualifications as protestant versions: married but once, not new convert, and should rule well his own household, keeping his children under control and perfectly respectful. I think the qualification of an elder proves the anointing of oil is not limited to Catholic priests.

Matrimony

The church requires a priest present for a valid Catholic marriage. The church requires a valid Catholic marriage and that grace will grow and help them with difficulties in the marriage. I believe a church may have membership rules. It is wrong to bind these rules with sin.

Holy Orders

This is the sacrament of the church when a man receives the powers of the priesthood. Priests are not allowed to marry: The church uses 1st Corinthians 7; 32=34 for the reason they don't allow priests to marry. I would like you to be free from concern as unmarried man is concerned about the Lord's affairs how can he please the lord. But a married man is concerned about the affairs of this world how can he please his wife and his interests are divided This is true as the word of The Bible is truth but I think it has caused the Catholic Church to have a shortage of priests and a lot of sexual morality problems.

The Catholic Church imposes church laws with all their sacraments some of these laws are mandatory , attendance every Sunday except for a serious reason, attend the holy days of obligation, confession and communion during the Easter Time between Ash Wednesday and AscensionThursday, and fasting and absence of meat every Friday During lent. These laws are called precepts of the church.. The church reserves the right to make and change these precepts at any time. It also teaches that anyone who fails to obey these laws commits mortal sin and only a Catholic priest can forgive these sins. The church may Have changed some of these precepts that I'm not aware of.

There is nothing in The Bible that States that it is a sin to disobey these church Laws. In my opinion this is adding to God's word which is the violation of revelations 22; 18 through 19, Which States we are not to add or detract from God's Word.

We should attend church often, as indicated in Hebrews 10; 25, let us not give up meeting together, as some are in the habit of doing, but let us encourage one another and all the more as you see the day approaching.

Attending church has many benefits but going to church doesn't give us salvation. If we miss a lot of church we will miss out on a lot of blessings.

6 Sins and Their Consequences

Sin is any willful thought or action that offends God. First John 5:17 says, "All wrong doing is sin, and there is sin that does not lead to death."

Repented sin is sin that does not lead to death.

Angels sinned before man was created.

And there was war in heaven. Michael and his angels fought against the dragon, and the dragon and his angels fought back. But he was not strong enough, and they lost their place in heaven. The great dragon was hurled down—that ancient serpent called the devil, or Satan, who leads the whole world astray. He was hurled to the earth, and his angels with him. (Revelation 12:7–9)

Then Adam and Eve committed the original sin when they ate from the tree of life. We inherit this sin when we are born. Romans 5:12–13 says, "Therefore just as sin entered the world through one man, and death through sin, and in this way death came to all men, because all sinned, for before the law was given, sin was in the world."

The Catholic Church teaches that water baptism takes away original sin. We know that only the blood of Christ can reconcile any sin by Romans 5:19: "For just as through the disobedience of one man (Adam) the many were made sinners, so also through the obedience of the one man (Jesus) the many will be made righteous."

We are purified by the blood of Jesus.

First John 1:7 says, "But if we walk in the light, as he is in the light, we have fellowship with one another, and the blood of Jesus, his son purifies us from all sin."

Are some sins worse than others? The Catholic Church classifies sins as venial or mortal. Actually, all sins are mortal because we cannot enter heaven with even a speck of sin on our souls. The differences in sins are how much it arouses God's displeasure. John 19:11 says, "Therefore he who handed me over to you is guilty of a greater sin."

This verse was Jesus's answer to Pontius Pilate when Pilate told Jesus he had the power to crucify him or release him. Jesus was probably indicating that Judas Iscariot was of greater sin than Pilate. I think this verse (John 19:11) does prove some sins displease God more than others. We classify denying the Holy Spirit as the worst sin because it is the only sin described in scripture as unforgiveable.

Jesus says in Matthew 12:32, "Anyone who speaks a word against the Son of Man will be forgiven, but anyone who speaks against the Holy Spirit will not be forgiven, either in this age or in the age to come."

Even though this verse was probably directed to the Pharisees, who publicly denied Jesus as the living Christ, it also applies to anyone who has heard the gospel of Jesus, but refuses to believe in him, blasphemes him, and refuses to believe in Jesus as the Christ (chapter 2).

Beware of religions that deny Jesus is God. I will expand on this in the chapter "Choosing a Church.".

We must not deny Jesus is God. We must also believe in the Trinity: Father, Son, and Holy Spirit.

By scripture we can believe that some sins displease God more than others. It would be impossible to label sins as to how much each one displeases God. We know God hates all sins, but scripture reminds us of several sins that must displease him severely.

Proverbs 6:16 lists six things that He hates, seven that are detestable to him. I interpret this as all seven of these are detestable.

A proud look

A lying tongue

Hands that shed innocent blood

A heart that devises wicked plans

A false witness who speaks lies

Feet that are swift to running to evil

One who sows discord among brethren

Psalm 5:5 says, "The arrogant cannot stand in your presence; you hate all who tell lies; bloodthirsty and deceitful men the Lord abhors."

Galatians 5:19–21 gives a list of sins that if anyone lives like this will not enter the kingdom of heaven. These sins are: "Sexual immorality, impurity and debauchery, idolatry, witchcraft, hatred, discord, jealousy, fits of rage, selfish ambition, dissensions, factions, envy, drunkenness, orgies, and the like."

God also gets very angry if we take advantage of a widow or orphan.

Do not take advantage of a widow or an orphan. 23 If you do and they cry out to me, I will certainly hear their cry. 24 My anger will be aroused, and I will kill you with the sword, your wives will become widows and your children fatherless. (Exodus 22:22–24)

The sin of adultery probably greatly displeases God as it can have an effect on marriages and possibly several other people

We don't know how God views these different sins, but I think most people would probably consider murder as one of the worst sins. Murder would also include the sin of abortion. These sins can have a horrendous effect on many people. We can imagine how distressful it would be to have a member of our family or someone close to us murdered.

Another reason murder can be so wrong is if the person hadn't accepted Christ, it eliminates the possibility. Murder usually has a devastating effect on a number of people.

Another sin that is detestable to the Lord is homosexuality. Leviticus 20:13 says, "If a man lies with a man as one lies with a woman, both of them have done what is detestable." Homosexuality is not only a detestable sin, but there are people applauding the gay marriage law. A lot of these people are not homosexuals and probably claim to be Christians but are applauding sin. We are to hate sin, not applaud it. I think most of these people probably have a friend or relative who is gay, and instead of admitting they're wrong, they condone it. I think these people will also be held accountable in some way. I am not saying that homosexuals can't repent and be forgiven. We need to pray for them. God will require a serious effort to change their lifestyle.

All sins can lead to death. "Lead to death" means if we continue to commit these sins and never repent and reject these sins, we will encounter death or hell. This means spiritual death, but some think this might also include physical death if they continue to live this lifestyle.

If we repent for our sins and do not continue to live a sinful lifestyle, we can be forgiven and know we have eternal life if we have accepted Christ.

First John 5:17–18 says, "All wrong doing is sin and there is sin that does not lead to death. We know that anyone born of God does not continue to sin; the one who was born of God keeps them safe and the evil one cannot harm them."

This was referenced in chapter 2.

Sin can also separate us from God and have an effect on how our prayers are answered. The following verses in Isaiah and Psalms appear to say the less we sin, the better God listens.

Isaiah 59:2 says, "But your iniquities have separated you from your God; and your sins have hidden his

face from you, so that he will not hear." Psalm 66:18 says, "If I had cherished sin in my heart, the Lord would not have listened."

We are to live our lives making every effort to stay away from sin. We are to hate sin as Paul tells us in Romans 12:9: "Love must be sincere. Hate what is evil; cling to what is good."

We are told to hate evil in Proverbs.

Proverbs 4:27 says, "Do not swerve to the right or to the left; Keep your foot from evil."

Proverbs 8:13 says, "To fear the Lord is to hate evil; I hate pride and arrogance, evil behavior and perverse speech."

Sometimes I think we use Romans 3:23, "For all have sinned and fall short of the glory of God," as an excuse to be lax about avoiding sin. People who live in sin and have family and friends living in sin tend to sweep sin under the rug with the idea that no one is perfect. This lifestyle is spiritually dangerous.

No one should wrong his brother or take advantage of him as the Lord says he will punish all such sins (1 Thessalonians 4:6). "The way of the Lord is a refuge for the righteous, but the ruin of those who do evil" (Proverbs 10:29).

7 Who Should We Confess Our Sins To

I didn't go to Catholic school, but I went to catechism taught by nuns every Saturday morning during the school year. I was in the eight-year-old class being prepared for our first communion class. We were probably studying confessing our sins to a priest when a boy asked if his non-Catholic relative could go to heaven. The nun's answer was only if his relative never committed a mortal sin because only a Catholic priest can forgive a mortal sin.

This question came up again in later years in a catechism class, and we heard the same answer. The old catechisms taught that priests were given the power to forgive sins, and they were the only way you could get a mortal sin forgiven. I am not sure what the church is teaching today, but it is still in a Vatican II updated catechism that priests can forgive sins. Jesus gave the apostles the power to forgive sins, heal the sick, and even raise people from the dead.

Matthew 10:5–8 says, "These twelve God sent out with the following instructions. Do not go among the Gentiles or enter any town of the Samaritans. Go rather to the lost sheep of Israel. As you go, proclaim this message: The kingdom of heaven is near. Heal the sick, raise the dead, cleanse those who have leprosy, and drive out demons."

Matthew 10:1 says, "He called his twelve disciples to him and gave them authority to drive out evil spirits and heal every disease and sickness."

I have found nowhere in scripture that powers like these were handed to anyone else or that anyone else was given the power to hand down these powers. Scripture does say the apostles ordained disciples, but this doesn't mean the powers Jesus gave the twelve were transferred on for generations. I have never seen a priest heal every disease and sickness or raise anyone from the dead.

Actually, the apostle Peter tells us that all believers are priests. First Peter 2:9 says, "But you are a chosen people, a royal priesthood, a holy nation, people belonging to God, that you may declare the praises of him who called you out of darkness into his wonderful light."

Jesus gave the apostles the power to forgive sins, but they weren't going to live forever. Scripture tells us how we can get forgiveness.

There are several Bible verses about forgiveness of sins. I will list some of them.

First John 1:9 says, "If we confess our sins, he is faithful and just and will forgive us our sins and purify us from all unrighteousness."

Acts 10:43 says, "All the prophets testify about him that everyone who believes in him receives forgiveness of sins through his name."

Acts 13:38 says, "Therefore, my brothers, I want you to know that through Jesus the forgiveness of sins is proclaimed to you."

Ephesians 1:7 says, "In him we have redemption through his blood, the forgiveness of sins, in accordance with the riches of God's grace."

Second Corinthians 5:17 says, "Therefore if anyone is in Christ, he is a new creation, the old is gone, the new has come."

Hebrews 8:12 says, “For I will forgive their wickedness and will remember their sins no more.”

These verses are telling us we need no one except Jesus to forgive our sins. Scripture does tell us we can confess our sins to each other so that you may be healed.

James 5:16 says, “Therefore confess your sins to each other and pray for each other so that you may be healed.”

Some theologians say this means to confess to someone you have injured or sinned against and pray for one another, that they may be healed. This has nothing to do with God’s forgiveness of our sins. We may also confess sins to someone we really trust or to our pastor. Catholic confession would be all right if the person didn’t believe the priest forgives the sins and that penance was not needed.

I have heard sermons that married people who have sinned against their spouses should confess to them. I think all the pastors warned the longer you wait, the worse it will be. This could be any sins of dishonesty, lying, secret gambling, illegal drugs, and infidelity. This could also include hiding a sin committed before the marriage that could have an effect on the marriage in the future. If we bring a lie into the marriage, it will probably eventually present a problem.

Proverbs 28:13 says, “He who conceals his sins does not prosper, but whoever confesses and renounces them finds mercy.”

I am relating this quote to spouses who are hiding sin. If they confess their guilt, their conscience shall be eased and their ruin prevented. I will give some examples of not confessing and hiding sin that can damage or even destroy marriages. I have heard more than one pastor say there are to be no secrets in marriage. Following are some examples.

If a wife doesn't know about a child her husband fathered before or during the marriage and years later the child shows up for reasons like they want to see their biological father or want some money for college, it would probably have a serious effect on the marriage. This might not cause a divorce, but I am sure the marriage will never be the same. I have seen cases similar to this.

Another example would be a wife who hides a sin of having a child or an abortion before marriage. This can also cause a lot of marriage problems. A child who was adopted out could also show up later in a marriage.

If an abortion is involved, there can be many ramifications from the abortion. I have read in the Right to Life Magazine that up to 80 percent of women who have an abortion will encounter some mental problems. Twenty-five percent need psychiatric counseling, some are suicidal, and divorce rates are high in these marriages. These women can also experience periods of irritability and be abusive to children. These women might also experience insomnia and other medical problems. You can learn more effects of abortion by Googling "abortion facts".

These bad effects of abortion can be detrimental to a marriage, and this person might be living in denial. I heard two Christian counselors on a radio show say that until a woman comes out of denial, she can't heal. This is why it is important for the husband to know so he can help get her the needed counseling. It seems as though troubled people need to be encouraged to get the help they need.

Families of these situations I have been describing will probably try and keep it a family secret. This is known as a “conspiracy of silence.” The cell phone dictionary defines it as: usually a secret or unstated agreement to remain silent among those who know something whose disclosure might be damaging, harmful, or against their own best interest or that of their associates.

Sometimes these secrets eventually come to surface in gossip circles. In trying to keep their family secret, at some point in time they probably will be deceitful. Psalm 5:6 says, “You destroy those who tell lies; bloodthirsty and deceitful men the Lord abhors.”

I am not saying that a person or a family needs to expose their sin to just anyone. I am saying not to be deceitful to the people it could have a serious effect on.

Sometimes it can be a very difficult decision whether to reveal the truth about someone. It might be best to consult a pastor.

8 How Should We Pray?

Praying is communicating by conversation with God, including praises, adoration, forgiveness, thanksgiving, and requests. Prayer should be our intimacy with God, a loving and personal relationship. We pray to any of the trinity as three are in agreement, but scripture usually tells us to pray to the Father in Jesus's name.

Colossians 3:17 says, "And whatever you do, whether in word or deed, do it all in the name of the Lord Jesus, giving thanks to God the Father through him."

John 14:13–14 say, "And I will do whatever you ask in my name, so that the son may bring glory in my name, and I will do it."

In the Sermon on the Mount Jesus said to pray in secret and don't babble like pagans.

Matthew 6:6–8 says, "But when you pray go into your room, close the door, and pray to your Father who is unseen. Then your Father who sees what is done in secret will reward you. And when you pray, do not keep on babbling like pagans, for they think they will be heard because of their many words, do not be like them, for your Father knows what you need before you ask him."

I think we have all been disappointed from time to time that God didn't answer our prayers in the way we wanted him to.

In the book of 1 John we can see it is very important that our requests be according to God's will, and in the book of James we are told not to ask for our own pleasures. So if you pray for a new fishing boat, your chances of getting it may be slim to none if you listen to God.

First John 14:15 says, “This is the confidence we have in approaching God: That if you ask anything according to his will, he hears us. And if we know that he hears us whatever we ask, we know that we have what we asked him.

Second thought on the fishing boat Jesus did like fishermen, so it could be his will.

James 4:3 says, “When you ask, you do not receive because you ask with wrong motives, that you spend what you get on your pleasures.”

The odds on the fishing boat just went back to slim to none.

We are told God hears the prayers of the righteous.

Proverbs 15:29 says, The Lord is far from the wicked but hears the prayers of the righteous.”

Proverbs 28:9 says, “If anyone turns a deaf ear to the law, even his prayers are detestable.”

John 9:31 says, “We know that God does not listen to sinners, He listens to the Godly man who does his will I think we can conclude that the less we sin, the better our prayers will be answered.

One might say we are all sinners so God doesn’t listen to us. This means God will hear the prayers of a person who has accepted Jesus as his or her Savior and who is living a Spirit-filled life. If a person hasn’t accepted Jesus as his or her Lord and Savior, his or her prayers are not heard. It is important to give God thanks and praise when our prayers are answered. I think we all have made the statement, “My prayers were answered." This might very well be true, but we should keep in mind that there could be other people praying for our petition that we didn't even know about. It could be friends, neighbors, relatives, coworkers, people at church, or someone you don't know. We might be surprised if we knew who was praying for us.

We should also pray for people we see in need. There are different ways we can pray. We can read prayers, or we can have our own conversation with God. Prayer is communicating with God, so I think God prefers a personal conversation. 1Thessalonians 5:16–18 tells us to pray continually, always giving thanks. Some say this means to be ready to pray at all times as we can't pray constantly.

We can pray quite often throughout the day because a prayer can be only a few words, such as, "Thank you, God," or "Lord, I need help with this." Constantly give God thanks and praise and give him the glory for everything good. You might be surprised by how much you can pray throughout the day even while doing your job.

Matthew 6:7 tells us not to babble like pagans because he knows what we need before we ask. I think this would include using repetitive prayers. Catholics have started what I call dialogue prayers, although the rosary is very repetitive. I know when I was a Catholic, when we prayed for something or somebody, we might say five Our Fathers, five Hail Mary's, and five Glory Bes. Saying the same prayers over and over isn't a personal conversation with God. I don't think this is the way God wants us to pray. I know Jesus gave the Lord's Prayer in the Sermon on the Mount, but I don't think Jesus intended for us to say it over and over for the same petition. When we are having a conversation with people, we wouldn't want them to keep repeating themselves over and over. Make your conversation with God like you are talking to a friend.

The most famous prayer is the Lord's Prayer Jesus gave us in the Sermon on the Mount, which is a prayer to God the Father. Jesus gave the disciples this prayer as a model prayer. This prayer gives us different areas we can pray for and add our own praises and petitions. Some of the following examples are from the Life Application Study Bible.

- Our Father who art in Heaven: Indicates that God is not only majestic and holy but also personal and loving.
- Hallowed be thy name: We praise and glorify God the Father in heaven and use his name respectfully.
- Thy kingdom come, thy will be done: God's work will be done and all evil is destroyed, and he will establish a new heaven and a new earth.
- Give us this day our daily bread: Every day God will provide for us what we need and the means to accomplish this purpose.
- Forgive us our debts as we also have forgiven our debtors: We ask God to forgive our debts. But we must also forgive others.
- And lead us not into temptation, but deliver us from the evil one. God will never lead us into temptation but will help us avoid Satan's temptations. He will not let us be tempted more than we can bear (1 Corinthians 10:13).

This is a model prayer, but for personal requests our own words could be more appropriate

Should we pray to Jesus for any of our petitions? Since God the Father gave Jesus all authority to judge sins, it would make sense to pray to Jesus for the forgiveness of our sins as well as God the Father.

John 16:23 tells us to ask the Father in Jesus's name; that seems to be praying to both Father and Son.

Proverbs 15:29 says, "The Lord is far from the wicked but hears the prayers of the righteous." I think this proverb indicates praying to Jesus.

Is it appropriate to pray to the Holy Spirit? Scripture tells us the three are in agreement (1 John 5:7–8). I think this scripture alone indicates we may pray to anyone of the trinity.

God gave us the gifts of the Holy Spirit. It would seem logical to pray to the Holy Spirit to reveal our gifts. Jesus told the disciples in John 14: 16–17, "I will ask the Father and he will give you another counselor to be with you forever, the spirit of truth." In times we need comforting we can pray to the (counselor) Holy Spirit.

A quote from Wayne Grudem's Systematic Theology: "It does not seem wrong to pray directly to the Holy Spirit at times, particularly when we are asking him to do something that relates to his special areas of ministry or responsibility."

No matter where we direct our prayers, God will answer them by his will, not by ours. When we pray, we should communicate in the following four areas:

1. Adoration:

I will exalt you my God the King; I will praise your name forever and ever. Every day I will praise you and extol your name forever and ever. Great is the Lord and most worthy of praise; His greatness no one can fathom. One generation will commend your works to another; they will tell of your mighty acts, they will speak of the glorious splendor of your majesty and I will meditate on your wonderful works. They will tell of the power of your awesome works, and I will proclaim your great deeds. (Psalm 145:1–6)

2. Confession:

If we confess our sins he is faithful and just and will forgive us our sins and purify us from all unrighteousness. (1 John 1:9)

Then I acknowledged my sin to you and did not cover up my iniquity. (Psalm 32:5)

This is the covenant I will make with them after that time, says the Lord. I will put my laws in their hearts, and I write them on their minds. Then he adds: their sins and lawless acts I will remember no more. And where these have been forgiven, there is no longer any sacrifice for sin. (Hebrews 10:16)

3. Thanksgiving and praise:

Always giving thanks to God the Father for everything, in the name of our Lord Jesus Christ. (Ephesians 5:20)

Be joyful always; pray continually; give thanks in all circumstances, for this is God's will for you in Christ Jesus. (1 Thessalonians 5:16–18)

4. Supplication or Petition:

Ask and it will be given to you; seek and you will find; for everyone who asks receives, he who seeks finds; and to him who knocks, the door will be opened. (Matthew 7:7–8)

Therefore, I tell you, whatever you ask for in prayer, believe that you have received it and it will be yours. (Mark 11:24)

"The righteous cry out, and the Lord hears them, he delivers them from all their -troubles. (Psalm 34:17)

If anyone of you lacks wisdom, he should ask God, who gives generously to all without finding fault, and it will be given to him. But when he asks, he must believe and not doubt, because he who doubts is like a wave of the sea, blown and tossed by the wind. That man should not think he will receive anything from the Lord, he is a doubled minded man, unstable in all he does. (James 1:5)

We should acknowledge all four of these areas in our daily prayers.

There is no certain order we have to pray in. I think it's only natural to give praise and thanksgiving when we get up in the morning. We need to thank God that everything went well throughout the night and praise him for a good morning even if the weather is not what we prefer or the baby cried a lot. We always need to keep in mind it could be worse. We should praise God for everything good. We should have a time of day for worship, including reading the Bible. The amount of scripture we read is up to us. Some people recommend about twenty minutes. I prefer smaller amounts and meditate on what it is saying to me, but I have an attention deficit problem.

We should confess our sins at night before or when we go to bed and also anytime we realize we have sinned. Repenting for sin is a huge part of Christianity. It is a must. Supplication or petition is what we are most likely not to forget. It is fine to ask for things, but we know it needs to be in God's will. This is a good time to add thanksgiving for answered prayer. We will probably forget to pray in all these areas at one time or another, but over time it will become a routine. I personally believe we don't have to be too methodical.

I have been quoting scripture about praying to God, but Catholics pray to Mary. First of all there is nothing in the Protestant Bible that says we can pray to Mary. I will quote some scriptures I think says it is wrong to pray to her.

Do not follow other gods, the gods of the people around you; for the Lord your God, who is among you is a jealous God and his anger will burn against you, and he will destroy you from the face of the land. (Deuteronomy 6:14–15)

The Catholic Church claims it does not worship Mary as a God. God says he is a jealous God, and when people are praying to Mary, they are leaving God out. The church claims she has some kind of power to go to God. That is what we have Jesus for.

We are not to pray to dead.

Let no one be found among you who sacrifices his son or daughter in the fire, who practices divination or sorcery, interprets omens, engages in witchcraft, or casts spells, or who is a medium or spiritualist or who consults the dead. Anyone who does these things is detestable to the Lord, and because of these detestable practices the

Lord your God will drive out those nations before you. (Deuteronomy 18:10–12)

Our practices are only to be with our God. I was listening to a Catholic radio call-in show when a man called in and quoted the verses about "Consults the dead. Anyone who does these things is detestable to the Lord." The call-in person asked how the church allowed praying to Mary when these verses forbid "consulting the dead." The radio host got emphatic and said, "That's ridiculous. We don't go to the cemetery like mediums and spiritualists and talk to our dead grandmother."

First of all, it's not ridiculous because there is a conjunction "or" between each type of person and it states "or" consult the dead. I think it is very clear we are not to consult the dead, and Mary is a dead person. She is not God.

I've read in an updated catechism (which meets the teachings of the Vatican II Council) that it is wrong to participate in spiritualism. The Catholic Church still teaches that they can pray to Mary and dead saints. Jesus respected his mother and obeyed her at the wedding of Cana, but he never put her on the same level as a god. The church claims they are not making her out to be a god.

When Catholics prays to Mary do they think they are the only one praying to her at this time? With Catholics all over the world praying to Mary, she could be receiving thousands of prayers in hundreds of different languages at the same time. She would have to be an omniscient God to process all these prayers.

You better not have strange gods before you. The gospel of Luke gives examples of Jesus regarding Mary as being on the same spiritual level as anyone who hears the word of God and obeys it.

Now Jesus' mother and brothers came to see him, but they were not able to get near him because of the crowd. Someone told him, "Your mother and brothers are standing outside wanting to see you." He replied, "My mother and brothers are those who hear God's word and put it into practice. (Luke 8:19–21)

Jesus didn't respond like Mary was anyone spiritually special as he put her on the same level as his brothers when he said, "They hear the word of God and put it into practice."

Luke 11:27–28 says, "As Jesus was saying these things, a woman in the crowd called out, "Blessed is the mother who gave you birth and nursed you."

He replied, "Blessed rather are those who hear the word of God and obey it."

Jesus is saying that the people who hear the word of God and obey it are also blessed.

Luke 1:46–49 says, "And Mary said: My soul glorifies the Lord and my spirit rejoices in God my Savior, for he has been mindful of the humble state of his servant. From now on all generations will call me blessed for the mighty one has done great things for me-Holy is his name."

The footnote in MacArthur study Bible for Luke 1:47 states:

Mary referred to God as "Savior" indicating both that she recognized her own need of a Savior, and that she knew the true God as her Savior. Nothing here or anywhere else in scripture indicates Mary thought of herself as "immaculate", (free from the taint of original sin).

Quite the opposite is true; she employed language typical of someone whose only hope for salvation is divine grace. Nothing in this passage lends support to the notion that Mary herself ought to be an object of adoration.

I asked a Catholic why he prayed to Mary, and the example he used was as a teenager if he wanted to use the car, he would have his mother to ask his dad for him because he knew his dad would more likely to allow him to have the car if she would ask. Using this analogy, he thinks God will answer his prayers better if he goes through Mary. This is using Mary as a mediator, but the Bible says that Jesus is the only mediator between God and man. First Timothy 2:5 says, "For there is one God and one mediator between God and men, the man Christ Jesus."

This says Mary cannot be a mediator between man and Jesus or a mediator between man and God the Father. Romans 8:34 states, "Christ Jesus who died-more than that who was raised to life is at the right hand of God and is also interceding for us."

We don't need Mary interceding for us because we have Jesus. Jesus said in John 14:6, "I am the way, the Truth, and the life, no one comes to the Father except through me."

The Protestant Bible has books that aren't in the Catholic Bible and they might have verses for praying to the dead. Protestant theologians omit these books because they don't line up with the basic books of the Bible. I quoted verses from Deuteronomy, the gospel of Luke, 1 Timothy, and Colossians, which are basic books.

There are books published about Mary making appearances throughout the world. The most popular appearance was to the three children at Fatima, Portugal. This could be Satan disguising himself as Mary because I think he likes people praying to her instead of God.

Second Corinthians 11:14 says, “And no wonder, for Satan himself disguises himself as an angel of light.”

The coming of the lawless one will be in accordance with the work of Satan displayed in all kinds of counterfeit miracles, signs and wonders, and every sort of evil that deceives those who are perishing. They perish because they refused to love the truth and so be saved. For this reason, God sends them a powerful delusion so they will believe the lie, and so that all will be condemned who have not believed the truth but have delighted in wickedness. (2 Thessalonians 2:9–12)

I think God was letting Satan send a powerful delusion. We know from the book of Job that sometimes God lets Satan do evil to people. We must remember that Satan is master of deception.

We must be aware that Satan sends powerful delusions. We should pray that we will recognize these delusions. The church teaches Mary’s body ascended into heaven. There is nothing in the Bible that states this actually happened. The church also teaches that people can pray to angels and saints. Colossians 2:18 and Revelations 19:9–10 forbid worshiping anyone besides God.

Colossians 2:18 says, “Do not let anyone who delights in false humility and the worship of angels disqualify you for the prize.”

Revelation 19:9–10 says, "Then the angel said to me, write: blessed are those who are invited to the wedding supper of the lamb! And he added, these are the true words of God. At this I fell at his feet to worship him, but he said to me, 'Do not do it! I am a fellow servant with you and with your brothers who hold to the testimony of Jesus. Worship God! For the testimony of Jesus is the spirit of prophecy.'"

In these verses the apostle John was overwhelmed by his vision and fell to the feet of the angel. The angel said, "Don't do it," because only God is worthy of worship.

The Bible forbids all worship except that of God. In Joshua 24:19 Joshua told the people God is a "Jealous God." Joshua went on to say in verse 20, "IF you forsake the Lord and serve foreign gods, then he will turn and do you harm and consume you, after he has done you good."

From these verses I have just quoted I think it is very clear we should only worship and pray to God.

9 Righteousness

Righteousness is the act of being godly, holy, pure, virtuous, and genuine. The sum total of this is all that is right and true. Our top priority should be to become like Jesus. We are never more like Jesus than when we are serving him. We should have love, joy, peace, patience, goodness, faithfulness, gentleness, and self-control.

We know that righteousness pleases God. If we want to be Christlike, we shouldn't hunger and thirst for the worldly ways and goods and keep our priorities straight.

Do not love the world or anything in the world. If anyone loves the world, the love of the Father is not in him. For everything in the world; the cravings of sinful man, the lust of his eyes, and the boasting of what he has and does, comes not from the Father, but from the world. The world and its desires pass away, but the man who does the will of God lives forever. (1 John 2:15–17)

This does not mean we can't enjoy physical things, but we are to avoid sins of the world. Lust is the desire for all evil things, not just sins of the flesh. We must guard our eyes so they don't lead us into sin.

God warns us about being led astray.

Dear children, do not let anyone lead you astray. He who does what is right is righteous, just as he is righteous. He who does what is sinful is of the devil, because the devil has been sinning from the beginning. The reason the Son of God appeared was to destroy the devils work. No one who is born of God will continue to sin, because

God's seed remains in him, he cannot go on sinning, because he has been born of God. This is how we know who the children of God are and who the children of the devil are: Anyone who does not do what is right is not a child of God; nor is anyone who does not love his brother. (1 John 3:7–10)

We must also avoid boasting and pride as Proverbs 16:18 says pride goes before destruction. Certain prides are permissible if we give all the glory to God. For example, I" am proud of my children that God gave me."

If we are to be Christ like we need to be forgiving of people who hurt us.

Matthew 18:21–22 says, "Then Peter came to Jesus and asked, Lord how many times shall I forgive my brother when he sins against me? Up to seven times? Jesus answered, I tell you not seven times, but seventy-seven times" (NIV).

I think forgiveness is one of the hardest teachings in Christianity. It seems as though it's only natural to want to retaliate when someone offends us. We need to remind ourselves the torture and sufferings Jesus went through for our sins and he forgives us.

If we ask Jesus to forgive our sins but do not forgive others who sin against us, we are like the man in the parable in Matthew 18.

Therefore, the kingdom of heaven is like a king who wanted to settle accounts with servants. As he began the settlement, a man who owed him ten thousand talents was brought to him, since he was not able to pay, the master ordered that he and his wife and his children and all that he had be sold to repay the debt. The servant fell on his knees before him. Be patient with me, he begged and I will pay back everything.

The servants master took pity on him, cancelled the debt and let him go. But when that servant went out, he found one of his fellow servants who owed him 100 denarii. He grabbed him and began to choke him. Pay back what you owe me, he demanded. His fellow servant fell to his knees and begged him, be patient with me, and I will pay you back. But he refused, instead, he went off and had the man thrown into prison until he could pay the debt. When the other servants saw what had happened, they were greatly distressed and went and told their master everything that had happened. Then the master called the servant in, you wicked servant he said, I cancelled all that debt of yours because you begged me to. Shouldn't you have had mercy on your fellow servant just as I had on you? In anger his master turned him over to the jailor to be tortured, until he should pay back all he owed. This is how my heavenly Father will treat each of you unless you forgive your brother from your heart. (Matthew 18:23–35)

If we want to be righteous, we must be forgiving people. There can be times we may stand our ground. Our pastor says,

"You don't have to be a doormat." In situations like this, we need to pray about it and maybe consult our pastor.

Besides forgiveness, our pastor gave four more steps of a righteous faith:

1. Resist peer pressure

2. Kindness and sacrifice

3. Tithing

4. Persevere in trials with a life of daily prayer

Acts of righteousness can help with our trials and challenges as we will encounter in our lifetime. We can find in scripture that we will have trouble.

John 16:33 says, "I have told you these things, so that in me you may have peace. In this world you will have trouble. But take heart! I have overcome the world."

We know we will have problems, but acts of righteousness can help get us through them and may even help avoid some of them. We will never be righteous enough not to have any challenges.

We might ask why God gives us these trials and why some people have a tremendous amount of problems and some people don't seem to have hardly any. I am not sure anyone has a complete answer for that, but 1 Peter 1:6–7 tells us problems can strengthen your faith and make it a greater worth:

Though now for a little while you may have had to suffer grief in all kinds of trials. These have come so that your faith of greater worth than gold, which perishes even though refined by fire, may be proved genuine and may result in praise, glory and honor when Jesus Christ is revealed.

Sometimes when we are not getting comfort in the fact that these blessings will be in heaven for eternity, we need to keep praying. Other reasons God might give us trials could be to get us on the right track, make us Christlike, or cause us to want a Savior. I will list several Bible verses that tell us that righteousness can help us through trials and troubles and help prevent them.

Proverbs 15:29 says, "The Lord is far from the wicked, but he hears the prayers of the righteousness."

Proverbs 11:28 says, "Whoever trusts in his riches will fall, but the righteous will thrive like a green leaf."

Proverbs 12:13 says, "An evil man is trapped by his sinful talk, but a righteous man escapes trouble."

Proverbs 11:8–9 says, "The righteous man is rescued from trouble and it comes on the wicked instead. With his mouth the godless destroys his neighbor, but through knowledge the righteous escape."

Proverbs 10:6 says, "Blessing crown the head of the righteous, but violence overwhelms the mouth of the wicked."

Psalm 34:19 says, "A righteous man may have many troubles, but the Lord delivers him from them all."

Psalm 91:14 says, "Because he loves me, says the Lord, I will rescue him; I will protect him, for he acknowledges my name."

Isaiah 54:14 says, "In righteousness you will be established: Tyranny will be far from you; you will have nothing to fear. Terror will be far removed" It will not come near you."

James 5:16 says, "Therefore confess your sins to each other so you may be healed. The prayer of a righteous man is powerful and effective."

We can see that righteousness should be a large part of our Christian walk but be careful and not to get self-righteous.

We might keep reminding ourselves of those five steps to a righteous faith.

10 Judge or Not to Judge

You have heard it said, “You can’t judge me; it’s in the Bible.” This is only partially true. This chapter is about what we can’t judge, what we can judge, and what we should judge cautiously.

I categorize judging into two categories: judging salvation and judging morals for restoring someone and protecting Christian values.

First, I will address judging someone’s salvation. We can’t judge salvation because only God can judge this. Sometimes we think we can judge people if they are living in sin or have lived in sin, but God the Father gave all authority to judge salvation to Jesus.

John 5:22 says, “Moreover the Father judges no one, but has entrusted all judgment to the son.”

If we try to judge someone’s salvation, we are trying to do God’s work. In Galatians 5:19–21, the apostle Paul gives a list of sins and says that those who live like this will not inherit the kingdom of heaven. Paul is talking in generalities. If we know of someone who commits any of these sins, we still can’t judge their salvation because we don’t know what’s in their hearts or what all Jesus takes into consideration.

Only God can judge what’s in people’s hearts as it states in 1 Kings 8:39, “God alone knows the hearts of men.”

We also don’t know what all Jesus will take into consideration. An example of this is what Jesus said as he hung on the cross. Luke

23:34 says, "Father forgive them for they do not know what they are doing."

From this verse I think Jesus will give special consideration for certain issues. People that might not know what they are doing could be one; people who have never heard the gospel, children who have died, people who have severe depression, those who are mentally handicapped, and those who are deceived by religious cults may be others. These are just a few examples.

Most of us probably think evil people like Hitler, Stalin, and their likes are probably going to hell. Even though there is an abundance of condemning evidence, we still should refrain from judging anyone's salvation. We could say that by all indications they are probably going to hell. Since God the Father gave all judgment to the Son (John 5:22), we shouldn't try to do God's work. Let Jesus do the judging, and don't dwell on these issues.

We should never want anyone to go to hell because God will use the same measure of judgment on us, and we all deserve hell and need Jesus for our Savior.

Matthew 7:1-2 says, "Do not judge or you too will be judged. For in the same way you will be judged and with the same measure you use, it will be measured to you."

An example could be if there is someone you don't want to be in heaven with, you probably won't be there either because you are judging harshly and God will use this measure of judgment and judge you harshly. I don't think any of us can afford harsh judgment.

Someone might say, "I am saved, so how will God judge me harshly?" If someone judges harshly, that would show lack of love and forgiveness; then God might judge the authenticity of his or her profession of faith. This is a hypothetical example.

There are Christians we can know are in heaven. Scripture tells us that martyrs for Jesus are in heaven.

Luke 9:24 says, “For whoever desires to save his life will lose it, but whoever loses his life for my sake will save it.”

We presume, unless there is evidence to the contrary, that people who confess with their mouth that Jesus is their Lord and Savior are going to heaven or if deceased are in heaven.

Romans 10:9 says, “If you declare with your mouth, Jesus is Lord and believe in you hear that God raised him from the dead, you will be saved.”

We also believe in the promise God gives us.

Titus 1:2 says, “A faith and knowledge resting on the hope of eternal life, which God who does not lie, promised before the beginning of time.”

So when a believer dies and we say they are in heaven, we are trusting in God’s promise as well as judging the person’s faith in Jesus.

Except for martyrs, we cannot positively know someone is in heaven because only God knows the heart. If it appears they professed a faith in Jesus, we presume they went to heaven.

The Old Testament acknowledges different people who are in heaven, like Enoch and all the prophets.

In the New Testament Jesus tells certain people that they have faith and will join him in heaven. The most popular example is probably the "good thief."

The apostle Paul tells us in 1 Corinthians 5:13 that God will judge those outside the church. We must only try to evangelize them. If we are going to evangelize, we first need to be sure the time and situation is right.

This is the advice of theologian Matthew Henry: "Council him and help him out, do not judge him. That if we presume to judge others, we may expect ourselves to be judged." (Reference to Matthew 7:1.)

I will quote the Bible verses when Jesus tells us to judge whether someone is ready for the gospel.

Matthew 7:6 says, "Don't give to dogs what is sacred; do not throw your pearls to pigs. If you do they may turn and tear you to pieces." Pearls in this verse represents the word of God.

This does not mean we are not to profess our faith. It means not to try and force the gospel on to someone who doesn't want to hear it.

I will quote the footnote from McArthur Study Bible for Matthew 7:6: "As the context reveals, this does not prohibit all types of judging. There is a righteous kind of judgment we are supposed to exercise with discernment. Censorious, hypocritical, self-righteous or other unfair judgments are forbidden, but in order to fulfill the commandments that follow, it is necessary to discern dogs and swine from our brethren."

The second type of judging mentioned at the beginning of this chapter is judging the morality and behavior of believers for restoring someone and protecting Christian values. We can definitely judge obvious sin listed in scripture. There are situations we should judge morals and sinful behavior, and there are times we should make sure our lives are in order before we judge someone else. None of us is sinless, so we need to be very cautious about judging people. I will list several scriptures that warn us about judging morals of believers.

Matthew 7:1-2 says, "Do not judge and you will be judged. Do not condemn and you will not be condemned. Forgive and you will be forgiven."

Do not judge or you too will be judged For in the same way you judge others, you will be judged, and with the same measure you use, it will be measure to you. Why do you look at the speck of sawdust in your brother's eye and do not pay attention to the plank in your own eye? How can you say to your brother, Let me take the speck out of your eye when all the time there is a plank in your own eye? You hypocrite, first take the plank out of your own eye and then you will see clearly to remove the speck from your brother's eye. (Matthew 7:1–5)

Jesus is telling us to examine our own lives first before we look at our brother's sin. The plank in our own eye means our sins, and the speck in our brother's eye means his sin is probably less than ours.

Jesus does say that if we get the sin out of our own lives, we may remove the speck from our brother's eye. We would need to be gentle and careful. Our pastor made the comment that by the time we get the plank out of our own eye, we might see that the speck in our brother's eye wasn't as bad as we thought.

The apostle Paul also warns us about judging in Romans 2:1-4:

You, therefore have no excuses, you who pass judgment on someone else, for at whatever point you judge the other you are condemning yourself, because you who pass judgment do the same things. Now we know that God's judgment against those who do such things is based on truth. So when you, a mere man, pass judgment on them and yet you do the same things, do you think you will escape God's judgment? Or do you show contempt for the riches of this kindness, tolerance and patience, not realizing that God's kindness leads you toward repentance?

When the apostle Paul says we do the same things, he doesn't necessarily mean the exact same sins, but we are all committing sins just as serious. Why should we immediately judge someone's sin when God is kind, tolerant, and patient to us? Paul says we are condemning ourselves.

Another good quote from Matthew Henry commentary, "That if we be modest and charitable in our censures of others, and decline judging them, and judge ourselves rather, we shall not be judged of the Lord." This corresponds to Luke 6:37.

Although we are warned many times about judging believing brothers, we may find it necessary to restore a brother caught in a sin as the apostle Paul explains in Galatians 6:1, "Brothers if someone is caught in a sin, you who are spiritual should restore him gently. But watch yourself or you also may be tempted."

If we decide to approach a believing brother about his sin, don't be shocked if he says it's none of our business. A lot of people don't realize that biblically it can be our business if we are concerned about their lives.

James 5:19–20 says, “My brothers, if one of you should wander from the truth and someone should bring him back, remember this: whoever turns a sinner from the error of his way will save him from death and cover over a multitude of sins.”

The apostle Paul tells us we are not to judge people outside the church but we can judge people inside the church.

But now I am writing to you that you must not associate with anyone who claims to be a brother or sister but is sexually immoral or greedy, an idolater or slanderer, a drunkard or swindler. Do not eat with such people. What business is it of mine to judge those outside the church? Are you not to judge those inside? God will judge those outside. “Expel the wicked person from among you!” (1 Corinthians 5:11–13)

Warn a divisive person once, then warn him a second time. After that have nothing to do with him. You may be sure such a man is warped and sinful; He is self- condemned. (Titus 3:10–11)

These are situations where the pastor and elders need to make the judgments. They have the right to expel. The church elders and/or the pastor need to judge the morals of people who are involved in the operation of the church and it starts with the elders (overseers) and deacons.

Now the overseer must be above reproach, the husband of but one wife, temperate, self-controlled, respectable, hospitable, able to teach, not given to drunkenness, not violent but gentle, not quarrelsome, not a lover of money. He must manage his family well and see that his children obey with proper respect. If anyone does not know how to manage his own family, how can he take care of God’s church?

He must not be a recent convert or may be conceited and fall under the same judgment as the devil. He must also have a good reputation with outsiders, so that he will not fall into disgrace and into the devils trap. Deacons, likewise, are to be men worthy of respect. Sincere, not indulging in much wine, and not pursuing dishonest gain. They must keep hold of the deep truths of the faith with a clear conscience. They must first be tested; and then if there is nothing against them, let them serve as deacons. (1 Timothy 3:2–10)

Anyone working in the church should be living the Christian faith. Churches need to be careful about people working in different ministries. If there is something erroneous in someone's past, then it would be for the elders and pastor to judge if it would have any ramifications to the position. If someone has a reason that they think someone shouldn't have a position in the church, they should consult an elder or the pastor.

Some of the most important judgments we need to make in our lives involve our family. We should judge our church's doctrine to make sure it is biblical and is right for the family.

If we have children, we need to teach them to associate with friends who have good morals. We should remind them to resist peer pressure that could get them in trouble. Peer pressure probably gets more children in trouble than any other reason.

Another important decision or judgment we make is when we choose who our spouse will be. One of the biggest misconceptions some people make is when they think they can change someone. An old saying is, "You can lead them to the altar, but you can't alter them."

The apostle Paul tells us not to marry an unbeliever in 2 Corinthians 6:14: "Do not be yoked together with unbelievers. For what do righteousness and wickedness have in common? Or what fellowship can light have with darkness?"

It is important to marry someone with similar moral and religious beliefs as it can cause problems in the marriage. I felt a need to write about this because I needed to know more biblical teachings before I got married, which contributed to the problems I described in the introduction to this book.

I know of split religion marriages that appeared fine, but I am sure it would have been better for the parents and the children if they went to the same church. This is why my wife and I decided to find one church.

When couples are getting serious in a relationship, they should discuss religious beliefs extensively. It is a good idea to know what religion each has on the first date because you might see a need not to continue this relationship. My wife and I needed to discuss our religions more extensively. It might have avoided a lot of religion problems early in the marriage.

It is not unusual to hear about someone getting bilked by a spouse claiming to be a Christian. Talk is cheap. Pray for guidance.

It takes prayer and communication to determine the direction for the spiritual growth of your family. The husband and wife may not have identical beliefs, but they should be close enough not to cause dissention in the marriage.

We have the right to put in place a standard of morals and beliefs for our family, but we don't have the right to try and force them onto other people. This is when we think everyone needs to believe just like we do. Some of the things this includes would be religious denominations, worship styles, parenting, mission trips, and political issues.

This doesn't mean we don't take a stand against obvious sins against God. An example would be abortion and same-sex marriage. We need to let people know we don't condone these sins. We need to judge the morals of our politicians and vote morals first. We don't want God to turn his wrath on this country like he did on Sodom and Gomorrah. Sometimes this is difficult to judge as some claim to be pro-life, but we don't see much action. We need to pray for guidance as how to vote.

Some people say that religion and politics don't mix, but abortion and same-sex marriage have become political issues, so they need to mix. Others say there are other important issues. There is no issue more important than this holocaust of killing over 55 million babies since Roe vs. Wade in 1973. This number is increasing as I write this. This is more than the total population of California.

I have read about and I personally know of a case when the doctors recommended an abortion because they said the baby would have serious defects. The mother refused to have an abortion, and the baby was born without any physical or mental defects.

As far as the safety of the mother, with the technology of cesarean section, a mother dying in childbirth is almost unheard of in this country. If these pro-choice people would witness a partial-birth abortion, I think they would change their minds. If they didn't they are as ruthless as the doctors who perform them.

In conclusion, we can judge what sins are by the list of sins in Galatians 5:19–21. We cannot judge people's salvations as only Jesus can do this (John 5:22). There are situations where we can and should judge morals and the conduct of people in the church. When we restore believers, we must not be hypocritical but have a sincere love for them even though we hate the sin.

Romans 12:9 says, "Love must be sincere. Hate what is evil; cling to what is good."

We should try to evangelize non-believers but we need to judge if they are ready to hear the word of God. If the time is not right to evangelize, we must stay at peace with them. Romans 12:18 says, "If it is possible as far as it depends on you, live at peace with everyone." Romans 12:21 says, "Do not be overcome by evil, but overcome evil with good." As Christians this can be challenging.

11 Giving Back to God

I am using the title "Giving Back to God" because everything belongs to God.

God tells us in Job 41:11, "Who has claim against me that I must pay? Everything under heaven belongs to me."

Our worldly ways make it easy to forget everything belongs to God. We have a title to our car, we have a deed to our property, and we have "our" 401K. When we check our bank account on the computer, we don't type in "God"; we use our user's name. So periodically I think we need to remind ourselves that everything does belong to God.

As a Catholic, I think the theory of giving was, it was between you and God, and give what you could afford. I never came close to tithing, and I had never heard a priest preach tithing. I did hear a priest say we should give until it hurts, and he did mention that Protestants give 10 percent. After leaving the church I learned about tithing from the Bible, and my wife believed in tithing.

I still struggled with it for several years, using excuses of medical bills and the cost of raising four children. I did not know for sure until we did our income tax and found out we were short of tithing. Our giving probably fell into a range from 6 to 9 percent.

I decided I needed to change my mentality and make tithing a priority and that tithing should be the minimum. I also needed to make this a cheerful priority, not a compulsion. Sometimes I still remind myself it is not compulsive and to be a cheerful giver. We won't lose salvation if we don't tithe, but will lose a lot of blessings.

I credit my mentality change to the Bible verses Malachi 3:6–12:

I the Lord do not change. So you the descendants of Jacob are not destroyed. Even since the time of your forefathers you have turned away from my decrees and have not kept them. Return to me, and I will return to you, says the Lord almighty. But you ask, "How do we rob you?" In tithes and offerings. You are under a curse, the whole nation of you because you are robbing. Bring the whole tithe into the storehouse. Test me in this says the Lord almighty, and see if I will not throw open the floodgates of heaven and pour out so much blessing that you will not have room enough for it. I will prevent pests from devouring your crops and the vines in our fields will not cast their fruit, says the Lord almighty. Then all the nations will call you blessed, for yours will be a delightful land, says the Lord Almighty.

God tells us in scripture that he loves a cheerful giver and we reap what we sow. The more generous we are, the more blessings we receive.

Whoever sows sparingly will also reap sparingly, and whoever sows generously will also reap generously. Each man should give what he has decided in his heart to give, not reluctantly or under compulsion, for God loves a cheerful giver. (2 Corinthians 9:6–7)

Tithing is not just Old Testament. Tithing is mentioned in Matthew 23 and Luke 11.

You give a tenth of your spices, mint dill and cumin, but you have neglected the more important matters of the law; justice, mercy and faithfulness. You should have practiced the latter, without neglecting the former. (Matthew 23:23)

But you ignore justice and the love of God. You should tithe, yes, but do not neglect the more important things." (Luke 11:42 Life Application study Bible)

Jesus is saying there are more important matters than tithing, but not to neglect it. Tithing is a way to give something back to God and show our faith.

Proverbs 3:9 says, "Honor the Lord with your wealth, with the first fruits of all your crops; then your barns will be filled to overflowing and your vats will brim over with new wine."

We can't buy our way to heaven, but Paul tells us to excel in giving in 2 Corinthians 8:7: "But just as you excel in everything, in faith, in speech, in knowledge, in complete earnestness, and in your love for us, see that you also excel in this grace of giving."

Statistics show that lower-income people give a higher percentage of their income than higher-income people. Jesus tells us that it's not the amount we give; it's the sacrifice we make.

Luke 21:3-4 says, "I tell you the truth, he said, this poor widow has put in more than all the others. All these people gave their gifts out of their wealth; but she out of her poverty put in all she had to live on."

If it is easy to pay the tithe, we should pay more. I was visiting with a man at a camp who told me he started a business at his home. His business grew so much that he had to move it out of his home. He eventually was shipping his product to other countries. He proceeded to tell me he was giving 40 percent to God. He said that God blessed him and that's what he decided to give back. I was impressed and probably needed to hear that.

If we are not tithing, try and work up to the tithe.

The Lord says, "Test me."

12 Indulgences

The Catholic Church teaches that an indulgence is the taking away of punishment due because of a person's sins.

The church teaches that you can gain indulgences for yourself and for people who are dead and whose souls are in purgatory. It teaches that you are granted different amounts of indulgences for prayers and the offering up of Catholic masses. The mass is the best indulgence.

Even in my early adolescence, I saw these prayers in the back of my prayer book with different number of days for indulgences. Some prayers had more days of indulgences than others. I wondered, where did these numbers come from, and how did anyone know if they were right?

In the preface of a Catholic Bible, I saw where indulgences were granted for reading the Bible. It said the number of days granted, but it didn't say how these numbers were calculated. I assume these calculations were made by popes who are supposed to be infallible.

I wrote about the infallibility of the popes in chapter 1. I see nothing in the Bible about indulgences or praying people out of purgatory, or that purgatory even exists.

A few years ago, I heard on a Catholic radio call-in station, a person called in and asked about praying for people in purgatory. The question was, "What happens if we are praying for people in purgatory and they have already been sent to heaven?"

The answer was that their prayers would be offered for someone else who was still in purgatory, probably someone who needed the prayers the most. How could anybody possibly know this? I have never seen anything in the Bible even close to this subject.

Since there is nothing in scripture about indulgences and praying people out of purgatory, I consider this adding to God's word. In the chapter on prayer, I quoted Revelation 22:18, which tells us we are not to add or detract from God's word.

At Catholic funerals, people can request masses to be said for the deceased, assuming they had to go to purgatory. With this request they pay some money for the priest to say the masses. Isn't this buying indulgences?

A rich person could get to heaven sooner by prearranging a lot of masses to be said after they die.

I went to a visitation and the priest gave a short message when he said there was no doubt in his mind that this person was in heaven. Later, I saw some people ordering masses to be said. I guess they didn't believe the priest.

Every person is accountable for themselves. Matthew 12:36–37 says, "But I tell you that men will have to give account on the Day of Judgment for every careless word they have spoken. For by our words you will be acquitted, and by your words you will be condemned."

Paul tells us in Romans 14:12, "So then each of us will give an account of himself to God."

I think these verses tell us we are on our own and we know that we need God's grace.

Hebrews 10:14–17 says, “Because by one sacrifice he has made perfect forever those who are being made holy. The Holy Spirit also testifies to us about this. First he says: This is the covenant I will make with them after that time, says the Lord, I will put my laws in their hearts, and I will write them on their minds. Then he adds: their sins and lawless acts I will remember them no more. And where these have been forgiven there is no longer any sacrifice for sin.” There would be no need for a purgatory.

13 Rituals

The Catholic Church has many rituals. Rituals do not give us salvation but in some instances produce blessings. I think some rituals are worthless. The ceremonies of baptism, communion, marriage, and anointing of oil to the sick are good, and we obtain blessings from these rituals.

Some rituals have no scriptural validity to them. On Holy Saturday the priest blesses water to be used for holy water throughout the year. This water is used for numerous things, including blessing themselves with the sign of the cross. Making the sign of the cross is good, but believing the water is holy is very controversial. I see nothing in the Bible that says a priest can make water holy.

The Old Testament gives instances of requiring water to clean unclean things with water to purify them. This not saying the water they used was holy. Matthew 3:11, says "Baptizing with water for repentance," but that doesn't mean the water was holy. It appears to me holy water is not biblical.

Another ritual there is no validity to would be the blessing of throats on St. Blaze Day. The priest crisscrosses two candles (not lit) under the chin and gives a blessing. I don't know why two candles. This blessing is supposed to help give immunity to diseases of the throat.

The story behind this was that a man named Blaze saved a child from choking; I guess this was considered a miracle so the church set aside a St. Blaze Day. I had doubts about this ritual as a teenager.

A Catholic ritual I consider a superstition is the use of incense around the casket at a funeral. I heard a priest say this was done in the early church to keep evil spirits away from the body and the church has continued this tradition. I don't see how this would keep evil spirits away and how could they hurt a dead body anyway. The soul is gone, and the body is nothing but future dust.

Could this be a pagan belief that creeped into Catholic doctrine during the rule of Constantine?

The wearing of a scapular is a ritual that a lot of Catholics probably don't know anything about. Scapulars were in our first communion packet.

Scapulars originated in monasteries. The very first scapulars originated as work clothes worn by the St. Benedict monks sometime in the time span of the seventh century. Some of the first scapulars were large pieces of cloth with a hole in the center and placed over the head. The front and the back would hang at equal distance on the chest and the back.

Over a period of time, they were made much smaller. There are various scapulars on the market through Catholic supplies with specific indulgences attached to them. There are eighteen different scapulars.

The most common scapular probably is one made with two pieces of cloth with a small picture of Jesus on one end and a small picture of Mary on the other end. These pictures are connected by two pieces of cord, and you put one picture on your chest and the other picture on your back. This is the type that was in my first communion packet.

The promise taught was that he who dies wearing this will be saved. This can't be true because the only thing that gives us heaven is our faith in Jesus for the grace of God by the shed blood of Jesus.

A ritual that I'm not sure how many churches do is the anointing of ashes on the forehead on Ash Wednesday. It symbolizes, "Dust thou art and dust thou shall return."

This is a good reminder, but a lot of churches don't do it.

A Catholic devotion I liked as a Catholic were the Stations of the Cross or Way of the Cross. This service was usually done during Lent. There are fourteen separate pictures or small statues on the wall around the church and numbered 1 through 14. Each station represents events in the crucifixion of Jesus.

The first station starts with Jesus being condemned to death, and the last station (fourteen) Jesus is laid in the tomb.

The prayers to Mary should be left out.

There was concern that some of the descriptions weren't biblically accurate, so in 1991 Pope John Paul II instituted a new series of the stations based on scripture alone. The reason I liked this devotion was because it gave the events that happened to Jesus on the way to the cross. As a child it gave me a better knowledge of the crucifixion.

The church has many more devotions and rituals, including benedictions and saying and singing of litanies.

The Catholic Church sells a lot of medals. Wearing a medal of Jesus or a cross is good, but a medal of Mary and or of different saints in my opinion is wrong because it is a form of worshiping someone besides God.

The Christian religion is all about Jesus.

14 The Rapture

Rapture is a term Christians use to describe Christians being taken into heaven before the end of times. The word rapture is not in the Bible, but what it stands for is.

Jesus describes it in Matthew 24:38–42:

For in the days before the flood, people were eating and drinking, marrying and giving in marriage, up to the day Noah entered the ark; and they knew nothing about what would happen until the flood came and took them all away. This is how it will be at the coming of the son of man. Two men will be in the field; one will be taken and the other left. Two women will be grinding with a hand mill; one will be taken and the other left. Therefore, keep watch, because you do not know on what day your Lord will come.

There is controversy among scholars about when the rapture will take place. Some think before the tribulation and some think after. As long as we know Jesus as our Savior, it doesn't make any difference when it happens.

Sometime after the rapture and tribulation will come the end of times.

Immediately after the distress of those days the sun will be darkened, and the moon will not give its light; the stars will fall from the sky and the heavenly bodies will be shaken. At that time the sign of the Son of Man will appear in the sky, and all the nations of the earth will mourn. They will see the Son of Man coming on the clouds of the sky with power and great glory. And he will send his angel with a loud trumpet call, and they will gather his elect from the four winds, from one end of the heavens to the other. (Matthew 24:29–31)

We must be ready as only God the Father knows when this will take place.

Matthew 24:36 says, “No one knows about that day or hour, not even the angels in heaven, nor the Son, but only the Father.”

15 What Is Heaven Like?

Heaven is a beautiful place of perfect happiness where God, angels, apostles, prophets, and saved people will be in the next world.

We think of heaven as being "up," as the following verses indicate. "After he said this, he was taken up before their eyes" (Acts 1:9). "While he was blessing them, he left them and was taken up into heaven" (Luke 24:51).

The apostle John's vision in Revelation 10:1 says, "Then I saw another mighty angel coming down from heaven"

Eventually, there will be a new heaven and a new earth. We know that God destroyed the earth's surface with the great flood except for Noah, his family, and a pair of animals of every kind in the ark. God promised he would never flood the world again. Genesis 9:11 says, "I establish my covenant with you: Never again will all life be cut off by the waters of a flood; never again will there be a flood to destroy the earth." God tells us in 2 Peter 3:7 that at the end of times the destruction will be by fire: "By the same word the present heavens and earth are reserved for fire, being kept for the day of judgement and destruction of ungodly men."

We know that only God the Father knows when the tribulation and the destruction will take place.

God promised us a Savior in Jesus, and He sent Jesus, who died for us. If we have Jesus in our life, we have nothing to fear. We can look forward to a perfect home. Second Peter 3:13 says, "But in keeping with his promise we are looking forward to a new heaven and a new earth, the home of righteousness."

Who will be in this new heaven and new earth? God will separate people as a shepherd separates sheep from the goats. He will put the sheep on the right, and they will go be with the Father in heaven. The people on the left (goats) will go to the abyss.

This judgment at the end of times is called the judgment of the nations. The final judgement is called the great white throne judgment.

There are different theories about how people will be judged. One theory is that everyone will be judged at the white throne judgement.

The most important thing is to be one of the sheep.

There will be a new heaven with a new earth, the home of righteousness. (2 Peter 3:13)

The new earth will have no seas. (Revelation 21:1)

In the apostle John's vision, he saw the Holy City, the New Jerusalem come out of the heaven. Then John heard a loud voice from heaven say, "Now the dwelling of God is with men, and he will live with them, they will be his people, and God himself will be with them and be their God" (Revelation 21:3).

The voice goes on to say (21:4), "There will be no more death or mourning or crying, or pain for the old order of things have passed away."

"He who was seated on the throne said, I am making everything new! Then he said, 'Write this down, for these words are trustworthy and true.' He said to me: It is done. I am the Alpha and the Omega, the Beginning and the End" (v. 5).

Verse 7 goes on to say whoever overcomes (accepts and believes in Christ) will inherit all of this. The murderers, immoral, idolaters, liars, and other unbelieving sinners will be in hell. This is called the second death.

One of the angels then took John and showed him the holy city coming out of heaven. Its brilliance was like a very precious jewel, like jasper, clear as crystal (Revelation 21:11).

The angel measured the city, and it was a cube, 12,000 stadia (1400 miles) in length, width, and height. This is almost two million square miles, which would be about three-fourths the size of the United States.

The walls were made of jasper and the city of pure gold. The foundations of the walls were decorated with twelve kinds of precious stones (v. 19).

This city also had streets of pure gold, like transparent glass, and a river with water clear as crystal. From this description we can certainly tell it will be beyond fascinating and how beautiful heaven will be.

Even though we don't know a whole lot about heaven, I will quote two scriptures we can depend on.

Now we know that if the earthly tent we live in is destroyed, we have a building from God, an eternal house in heaven, not built by human hands. (2 Corinthians 5:1)

In my Father's house are many rooms; if it were not so, I would have told you. And if I go and prepare a place for you, I will come back and take you to be with me that you also may be where I am. (John 14:2–3)

After someone passes away I have heard statements like, “They are probably looking down watching events happening here on earth.” I don’t think we see or know anything that happens on earth. Heaven wouldn’t be perfect happiness if we could see or know anything that’s happening on earth.

I think this is verified by Isaiah 65:17: “Behold, I will create new heavens and a new earth. The former things will not be remembered nor will they come to mind.”

If we could remember earth, we would be sad if a loved one wasn’t in heaven. I know there are people who think everyone goes to heaven. If they would read the Bible, they would know this is not true. If a loved one isn’t in heaven, we won’t remember they even existed, as Isaiah said, “nor will they come to mind.”

The Sadducees questioned Jesus about the wife who had seven husbands. Whose wife would she be at the resurrection?

They thought they had Jesus in a trap, but Jesus told them at the resurrection people will neither marry nor be given in marriage. They will be like angels in heaven (Matthew 22:30).

Scripture tells us we will be given a new body when we go to heaven in 1 Corinthians 15:40: “The splendor of the heavenly bodies is one kind, and the splendor of the earthly bodies is another.”

The apostle Paul expands on this by saying our earthly body is perishable but our raised body will be imperishable (1 Corinthians 15:42). “I declare to you brothers that flesh and blood cannot inherit the kingdom of God, nor does the perishable inherit the imperishable” (v. 50).

I think it is conceivable to believe our new bodies will be like Jesus's body after the resurrection.

Philippians 3:21 says, "Who by the power that enables him to bring everything under his control, will transform our lowly bodies so that they will be like his glorious body.

Jesus's body was definitely different after the resurrection as he entered rooms with locked doors two times. The second time he told the doubting Thomas to, "Put your finger here, see my hands. Reach out your hand into my side, stop doubting and believe" (John 20:27).

Thomas said to him, "My Lord and my God!" (v. 28).

Since Thomas could put his hand into Jesus's side, there obviously was no blood or pain. His body must have been transformed, but he was still recognizable and his body must have been intact.

Since Philippians 3:21 says he will transform our bodies like his glorious body, I think we can conclude we will recognize people in heaven and people in heaven will recognize us, because the disciples recognized Jesus after the transformation of the resurrection.

It appears that at the transfiguration Peter, James, and John recognized the great prophets Moses and Elijah, whom they never knew. Since the apostles never knew the prophets before, this could indicate that we will recognize people we didn't know, but heard about.

Then is it possible that we will recognize famous people from many years ago, and could it start with Adam and Eve and go down through history? I don't think anyone could have the answer to this, but it could make some interesting conversation.

The most important attribute of heaven is being with God and his glory. This is the ultimate!

We must have our name in the Book of Life in order to enter the kingdom of heaven. Revelation 20:15 says, "If anyone's name was not found written in the Book of Life, he was thrown into the Lake of Fire."

The last chapter of this book will tell how to get your name into God's Book of Life.

16 What Is Hell?

Hell is a place you don't want to go. It is severe punishment for eternity and usually referred to as the "fire of hell."

There is some controversy whether hell is actually fire. Most Bible verses refer to it as fire or burning sulfur.

Luke 16:23–24 says, "In hell, where he was in torment, he looked up and saw Abraham far away, with Lazarus by his side, so he called to him, 'Father Abraham, have pity on me and send Lazarus to dip the tip of his finger in water and cool my tongue, because I am in agony in this fire.'"

The Lazarus in this story is not the Lazarus who was Jesus's friend who he raised from the dead. I would consider this story a parable to illustrate the agony of hell.

Jesus also said in Mark 9:43, "If your hand causes you to sin, cut it off. It is better for you to enter life maimed than with two hands to go into hell, where the fire never goes out."

Revelation 14:10–11 says, "He will be tormented with burning sulfur in the presence of the holy angels and of the lamb. And the smoke of their torment rises forever and ever …"

Matthew 26:24 is another Bible verse that tells us how terrible hell is: "But woe to that man who betrays the Son of Man! It would be better for him if he had not been born."

These next verses explain what Jesus will do at the last judgment.

Matthew 25:41 says, "Then he will say to those on his left, 'Depart from me, you who are cursed, into the eternal fire prepared for the devil and his angels."

Matthew 25:46 says, "Then they go away to eternal punishment, but the righteous to eternal life."

What kind of people go to hell? Here is a list.

1Corinthians 6:9–10 says, "Do you not know that the wicked will not enter the kingdom of God? Do not be deceived: Neither the sexually immoral nor idolaters nor adulterers nor male prostitutes nor homosexual offenders nor thieves nor the greedy nor drunkards nor slanderers nor swindlers will inherit the kingdom of God."

In hell people will probably be fighting among themselves, blaming someone for them being there as they also experience the physical pain.

Luke 13:28 says, "There will be weeping there, and gnashing of teeth, when you see Abraham, Isaac, and Jacob and all the prophets in the kingdom of God, but you yourselves thrown out." I think this is a good indication that people in hell know who is in heaven, but I don't think people in heaven know who is in hell. This is also another indication we will recognize people in heaven that we never knew.

Too many people think they just need to be a good person to get heaven. This next Bible verse says differently. John 14:6 says, "I am the way the truth and the life. No one comes to the Father except through me (Jesus)."

There will be people who lived a basically good life but will go to hell because they never accepted Jesus as their Lord and Savior. It will really add to their suffering if they learn that someone like Jeffrey

Dahmer, a notorious killer, is in heaven because he accepted Christ before he was killed in prison. I have heard of people that say if our God judges like that, they don't want any part of this God. I am not about to criticize God's system, and these people are in for a rude awakening.

There is a book called Jeffrey Dahmer's Story of Faith written by Greg Taylor, which tells how Dahmer was led to faith in Jesus before he was killed. Accepting Jesus as your savior will save you from the agony of hell. Jesus said in the Sermon on the Mount that only a few will enter the gate to life (Matthew 7:14).

17 Selecting a Church

I wrote in the preface that my family needed one church for the whole family. Sometimes it takes a while to find a church that fits the needs of the whole family.

We found a nice small church, but after a few years, we decided we needed a larger church that would have more to offer our children.

We started going to a larger church of the same denomination. We went to this church for several years until it started to make changes. We didn't like some of the changes that ensued and then changed to even a larger church still of the same denomination. We have been going to this church for several years, and it seems to be a fit.

It is important that the husband and wife both like the church they are attending. This could mean that both sides might have to give a little. This is better than going to separate churches as my wife and I did early in our marriage. From my experience these are the guidelines I recommend for selecting a church.

Does the pastor preach strong biblical teachings?

Do the church leaders appear to be friendly and godly people?

Does the church support missions and reach out to the community?

Are the people friendly, or are there groups of cliques?

If you have children, do you like their youth programs?

Is the music the kind you prefer?

It would probably take a few visits to answer these questions, and keep in mind you won't find a perfect church. Music is an important issue to many people, including myself. There seems to be a consensus that traditional and contemporary music don't mix.

In my opinion, I think they do mix. I guess most people disagree with me because there probably aren't many churches that have both at the same service. I think traditional hymns send more of a salvation message and contemporary praise songs are more glorify and praise God songs. Sometimes one of our worship leaders will have both types, and it seems as I feel more presence of the Holy Spirit. Large churches sometimes offer a service in each style.

Check out the church's position on abortion. This is a big issue in our society today. I think most churches consider the fetus a human life and that abortion is a serious sin, but make sure. I want my church to take a strong position against abortion, not for it to be a subject they prefer not to talk about.

I really get irritated over the double standard of giving the mother the choice of whether her fetus is a person. Abortion is a serious sin, but Jesus will forgive those who repent just as God forgave Paul for his participation in murders.

Another controversial issue is homosexuality. Homosexuality is a sin and detestable to God. First Corinthians 6:9–10 says, "Do you not know that the wicked will not inherit the kingdom of God? Do not be deceived: Neither the sexual immoral nor idolaters nor adulterers nor male prostitutes nor homosexual offenders nor thieves nor the greedy or drunkards nor slanderers nor swindlers will inherit the kingdom of God."

Leviticus 20:13 says, "If a man lies with a man as one lies with a woman, both of them have done what is detestable."

We are all sinners, but we should not take a weak approach to sin. I want my church to teach a strong gospel and not one that is watered down.

There are churches that speak in tongues in their services. This is a matter of preference and has nothing to do with salvation.

The apostle Paul states in 1 Corinthians 14:18–19, "I thank God that I speak in tongues more than all of you. But in a church, I would rather speak 5 intelligible words to instruct others than 10,000 words in a tongue."

Paul gives an example how speaking in tongues during a service might not be good in 1 Corinthians 14:23–25:

So if the whole church comes together and everyone speaks in tongues, and some who do not understand or some unbelievers come in, will they not say that you are out of your mind? But if an unbeliever or someone who does not understand comes in while everybody is prophesying, he will be convinced by all that he is a sinner and will be judged by all, and the secrets of his heart will be laid bare. So, he will fall down and worship God, exclaiming, God is really among you!

These verses I have just quoted are the reason I don't prefer this type of church, but it's your choice.

Before deciding on a church, it's a good idea to visit with a pastor and ask questions about the church. Make sure the church is a Bible teaching church in that Jesus is God, the second person of the Trinity, and he is the only way to heaven.

John 14:6–7 says, “I (Jesus) am the way and the truth and the life. No one comes to the Father except through me. If you really know me, you would know the father as well. From now on you do know him and have seen him.”

The church must also teach the Trinity, Father, Son and Holy Spirit. First John 5:7–8 (NKJV) says, “For there are three that bear witness in heaven: The Father, the Word, and the Holy Spirit, and these three are one. And there are three that bear witness on earth: The spirit, the water, and the blood; and these three agree as one.”

Matthew 28:18–20 says, “And Jesus came and spoke to them saying, all authority has been given to me in heaven and on earth. Go therefore and make disciples of all nations, baptizing them in the name of the Father and to the Son and of the Holy Spirit, teaching them to observe all things that I have commanded you, and Lo, I am with you always, even to the end of the age” (NKJV). Amen.

Make sure the church teaches that Jesus is both God and man. Some religions and cults teach that Jesus is just a divine son and not actually God. Jesus came to earth as a man but still had godly powers. These churches and cults that deny Jesus is also God are guilty of blasphemy.

Colossians 2:8 says, “See to it that no one takes you captive through hallow and deceptive philosophy, which depends on human traditions and the basic principles of this world rather than on Christ.” There is a denomination that uses a small-case g in their Bible in the word God in John 1:1, “And the word was ‘God.’”

They say this means that Jesus isn't the almighty God. Their Bible is the only Bible I know of that uses the small-case g in the word God in this passage.

They are condemning themselves because we are only to worship the one and only God and not have any other gods before us. Deuteronomy 6:14–15 says, "Do not follow other god's, the God's of the people around you; for the Lord your God, who is among you, is a jealous God and his anger will burn against you, and he will destroy you from the face of the land."

This is the scripture I was referring to that tells us Jesus is God. John 1:1–3 says, "In the beginning was the word, and the word was with God and the word was God. He was with God in the beginning. Through him all things were made, without him nothing was made that has been made." Keep in mind "the word" means Jesus.

I will quote some verses from Proverbs that reiterate what John 1:1–3 proclaims.

I have been established from everlasting, from the beginning, before there was ever an earth. When there no depths, I was brought forth, when there were no fountains abounding with water.

Before the mountains were settled, before the hills, I was brought forth; While as yet he had not made the earth or the fields, or the primal dust of the world. When he prepared the heavens, I was there. (Proverbs 8:23–27 NKJV)

These religions that teach Jesus is just a divine son usually try and impress us with how they focus on the family and how happy they are. Good family life is important, but Jesus as God must be the center of our family. There are no perfect churches, but try and find one that teaches strong biblical truths and fits your family needs even though it might not be close to home. A good church is worth the drive.

It is important to go to church as often as possible. Hebrews 10:25 says, "Let us not give up meeting together as some are in the habit of doing, but let us encourage one another and all the more as you see the day approaching." "As you see the day approaching" refers to the second coming of Christ, the end of times.

Going to church helps keep us accountable.

In the chapter on works I emphasized the importance of the father taking his family to church. Single people also need the benefits of going to church with all the temptations in the world and to help them with their walk with Christ.

We also need to fellowship and worship with like believers in this carnal world.

It is a good idea to belong to a small group to get to know likeminded believers better and maybe be able to comfort or aid someone in a challenging situation, or they might help you in a challenging situation. The best comfort for hurting people is prayers. I have seen many prayers answered in life groups.

Galatians 6:2 says, "Carry each other's burdens."

Going to church on a regular basis will help us be the Christians we ought to be and hopefully keep us from backsliding. There also may be a sermon we need to hear. Missing church can develop into a bad habit.

18 Summary of Important Teachings

The purpose of this book was to be a guide for Catholics, nonpracticing Catholics, and nonbelievers for what they need to know and believe to be saved. I gave my opinion of what a church should teach and what to look for in a church, and I hope it will be helpful for others in their walk with Christ.

I think it is important to know that the apostle Paul persecuted Christians and God's church before he accepted Christ and wrote several epistles in the New Testament. I think this is important because it is a testament that we all can accept Jesus no matter how many sins we have committed, except someone who has blasphemed Jesus after they understood the gospel. The apostle Paul was ignorant about the gospel of Jesus, which was why he could accept Christ. He was not ignorant any longer as he became a prolific writer of the New Testament. All writers of the Bible received their wisdom from God as the Bible is God breathed (2 Timothy 3:16).

All of our prayers should be directed to only God the Father, God the Son, and the Holy Spirit. We pray in Jesus's name when we pray to the Father. Jesus is the only mediator between man and God (1 Timothy 2:5). We can also pray to the Holy Spirit preferably in his area of counseling and comforting.

Some churches have sacraments, which are works, so we do not receive salvation by doing sacraments. If we could be saved by works then Jesus suffered and died for nothing. Jesus paid the full price for our sins on the cross. Hebrews 10:17–18 says, “Their sins and lawless acts I will remember no more. And where these have been forgiven, there is no longer any sacrifice for sin.”

Because only God know the hearts of man and God gave full authority to judge to Jesus, we should not try and judge someone’s salvation. We can and sometimes should judge morals of behavior but should only evangelize nonbelievers and gently counsel believers if we are living the Christian faith ourselves.

I will give several passages of scripture that make a good foundation for a faith in Jesus Christ.

Probably the most famous verse in the Bible is John 3:16, and verses 17 and 18 are also very important.

John 3:16 says, “God so loved the world that he gave his one and only Son, that whoever believes in him shall not perish, but have eternal life.”

A. God so loved the world that he gave his only one and only Son.

1. To pay for Adam and Eve’s sin and for all future sins.

2. God promised this Savior in the book of Genesis.

Genesis 3:15 says, “And I will put enmity between you and the woman, and between your offspring and hers, he will crush your head, and you will strike his heel.”

Your offspring means Satan and unbelievers.

Her offspring means believers in Christ.

Crush your head means Jesus defeats Satan when he is resurrected.

Strike his heel means Satan's attempt to defeat Jesus.

John 3:17 says, "For God did not send his Son into the world to condemn the world, but to save the world through him."

A God promised a savior in Genesis, but God also had it prophesied through many of the prophets in the Old Testament. Three important ones are Zechariah 9:9, Micah 5:2, and the most important one, the entire chapter of Isaiah 53.

This next verse is also very important.

John 3:18 says, "Whoever believes in him is not condemned whoever does not believe stands condemned already because he has not believed in the name of God's one and only Son."

Now God sent his Son to save the world not to condemn, but we must truly believe in him, trust in him, and commit to him for everlasting life. This is more than just knowing who Jesus is.

Can people know you are Christian without you telling them? If you were arrested for being a Christian, would there be enough evidence to convict you?

Verse 18 states, "Whoever does not believe stands condemned already."

This is very strong language that too many people are ignoring.

Matthew 7:13 says, "For wide is the gate and broad is the road that leads to destruction, and many enter through it."

Another very important salvation verse is Romans 10:9, which tells us to "confess with our mouth Jesus is Lord." We are not to keep

Jesus a secret like we are ashamed of him because, "Anyone who trusts in him will never be put to shame."

It is also absolutely necessary to, "Believe in your heart that God raised him from the dead." God the Father raised Jesus from the dead because the sacrifice was complete and Jesus was God according to the prophecy of the prophets.

One of the most important verses in the entire Bible is Ephesians 2:8. It tells us we are saved by grace through faith, not by works. Works are fruits of our faith.

Scripture tells us, "There is one God and one mediator between God and men, the man Christ Jesus" (Timothy 2:5).

I will offer more important scriptures to know for your walk with Christ. John 14:6 says, "Jesus answered, 'I am the way the truth and the life. No one comes to the father except through me.'"

We must accept Jesus before we can go to the Father. Paul emphasizes in the book of Romans that sin is death, but Jesus died for our sins so we might have eternal life. Romans 6:23 says, "For the wages of sin is death, but Jesus died for our sins so we might have eternal life in Christ Jesus our Lord."

We must believe in Jesus to be saved and these next verses emphasize this.

John 11:40 says, "Jesus said to her, did I not say to you that if you believe, you would see the glory of God."

First John 3:23–24 say, "And this is his command: To believe in the name of his son, Jesus Christ, and to love one another as he commanded us. Those who obey his commands live in him, and he in them. And this is how we know that he lives in us: We know it by the spirit he gave us."

I will give the quote from the footnotes of MacArthur Study Bible for John 3;23-24, page 1970.

These verses again repeat the three features of this epistle; believing, loving, and obeying—which are the major evidences of true salvation.

In the footnotes MacArthur also gives the three benefits of love for the true Christian. They are assurance of salvation, answered prayer, and the abiding presence and empowering of the Holy Spirit.

It is important to know we are saved. It shows that we trust in the word of Jesus. A daily routine of prayer and studying scripture will build a strong faith in Jesus and help us live our faith. We must live our faith and walk as Jesus did if we claim to be a follower of Christ (1 John 2:6).

First John 5:13 says, "I write these things to you who believe in the name of the Son of God so that you may know that you have eternal life."

We need to remember Jesus has plenty of grace. It never runs out, but we must believe in Jesus, repent, and have faith.

If we don't know Jesus as our Lord and Savior, we are living in darkness. First John 1:5 says, "This the message we have heard from him and declare to you: God is light; in him, there is no darkness at all."

We should also remember John 15:5 tells us without Jesus we are nothing. Without him our prayers will not be answered, and we will not bear good fruit and receive his blessings.

Of all of the apostles' writings, I think the gospel of John and his three epistles convey a profound message for believing, accepting, repenting, and trusting in Jesus for salvation. The apostle John tells us we can secure our salvation. The next verses are good to know when someone is teaching something that isn't in scripture either by adding or detracting.

I warn everyone who hears the words of the prophecy of this book: If anyone adds anything to them God will add to him the plagues described in this book.

And if anyone takes words away from this Book of Prophecy, God will take from him his share in the tree of life and in the Holy City, which are described in this Book. (Revelation 22:18–19)

We must believe in the Bible, nothing more, nothing less!

If we don't want to be in darkness and the fire of hell in the next life, we must make sure our name is in the Book of Life.

Revelation 20:15 says, "If anyone's name was not found written in the "Book of Life", He was thrown into the lake of fire."

If you profess your faith in Jesus with all your heart and let your faith produce good works, your name will be in the Book of Life.

Here are five steps to professing your faith in Jesus.

1. Acknowledge I/we are all sinners.

2. Repent, face God and change your life and repent for your sins.

3. Believe Jesus Christ is God and that he died or our sins and God the Father raised him from the dead.
4. Make the decision to profess your faith in Jesus and accept him as your Savior.
5. Believe in the Trinity, Father, Son, and the Holy Spirit. We must believe there are three persons in one God.

I will give some verses that say the three are God.

God the Father—Genesis 1:1, "In the beginning God created the heavens and the earth."

God the Son—John 1:1–2, "In the beginning was the Word (Jesus), and the Word was with God, and the Word (Jesus) was God, He was with God in the beginning."

God the Holy Spirit—Acts 5:3–4, "Then Peter said, "Ananias, how is it that Satan has filled your heart that you have lied to the Holy spirit—You have not lied to men but to God."

When we say Jesus died for our sins, this means he made it possible for us to enter the kingdom of heaven. We cannot enter heaven with even a micro speck of sin. It had to be a perfect sacrifice for our sins, and only Jesus could accomplish this. No other human could withstand the suffering Jesus had. If we believe in Jesus with our whole hearts and that he died for our sins, he makes our souls pure, which we cannot do on our own.

This does not mean we won't endure some challenges and some consequences from our sins. Righteousness can help us endure our challenges (Psalm 34:19).

We should develop a daily routine of praying during the day even if it is only a few words. Be repentant, forgiving, and thankful, and give God all the glory for everything good. Get equipped by studying and meditating on the word of God.

The amazing thing about God is if we fail today, we can always start over!

Reference sources:

N. I. V. Bible. Oxford University Press Inc. Copyright 1984 by Zondervan Corp.

Chronological Life Application Study Bible, N,L,T. Tindale House Publishers Inc.

Carol Stream, Illinois.

Copyright 1988. Ref. page 1331.

MacArthur Study Bible, N.K.J. Word Publishing, a division of Thomas Nelson Inc, Nashville

Tennessee. Copyright 1997. Ref, pages: 1930,1512,1404,1970.

Matthew Henry Commentary. Zondervan Publishing, Grand Rapids, Michigan.

Copyright 1961. Ref. pages: 1287, 1287, 1934,762, 1233, 1233.

J. Vernon McGee. Thru the Bible Commentary Series, Epistle James. Published by Thomas Nelson, Inc. Nashville, Tennessee. Copyright 1991.Ref. pages;65and64.

Wayne Grudem. Systematic Theology. Zondervan Publisher, Grand Rapids, Michigan.

Copyright 1994. Ref. pages; 710 and 381

Wayne Grudem, Christian Beliefs. Published by Zondervan Publishers Inc. Grand Rapids, Michigan. Copyright 2005. Ref. page 184.

The New Book of Knowledge Encyclopedia. Book 16. Grolier Inc

Copyright 1966. Ref. pages 296 and 297.

Carol Wimmer. Author of the poem When I Say I am a Christian.

Copyright 1988

Wikipedia-internet encyclopedia. A free encyclopedia written by people who use it.

All quoted Bible verses are Niv 1984 version unless indicated otherwise.

www.ingramcontent.com/pod-product-compliance
Ingram Content Group UK Ltd.
Pitfield, Milton Keynes, MK11 3LW, UK
UKHW041822200726
13854UKWH00001BA/492